Abraham Lincoln

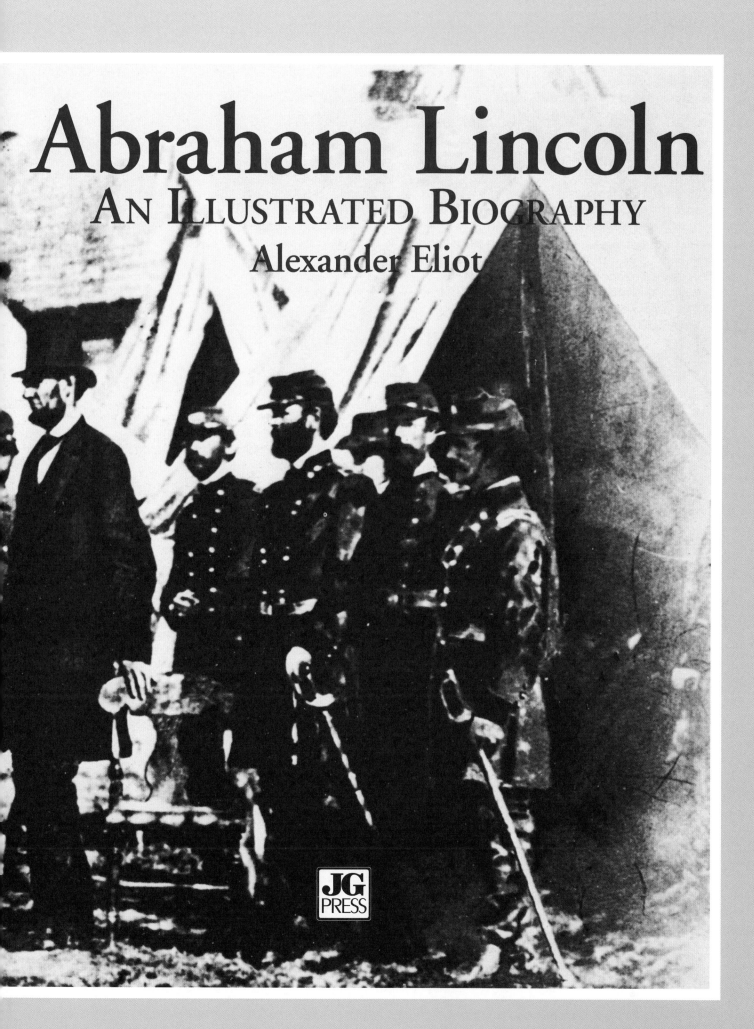

Abraham Lincoln
AN ILLUSTRATED BIOGRAPHY
Alexander Eliot

JG PRESS

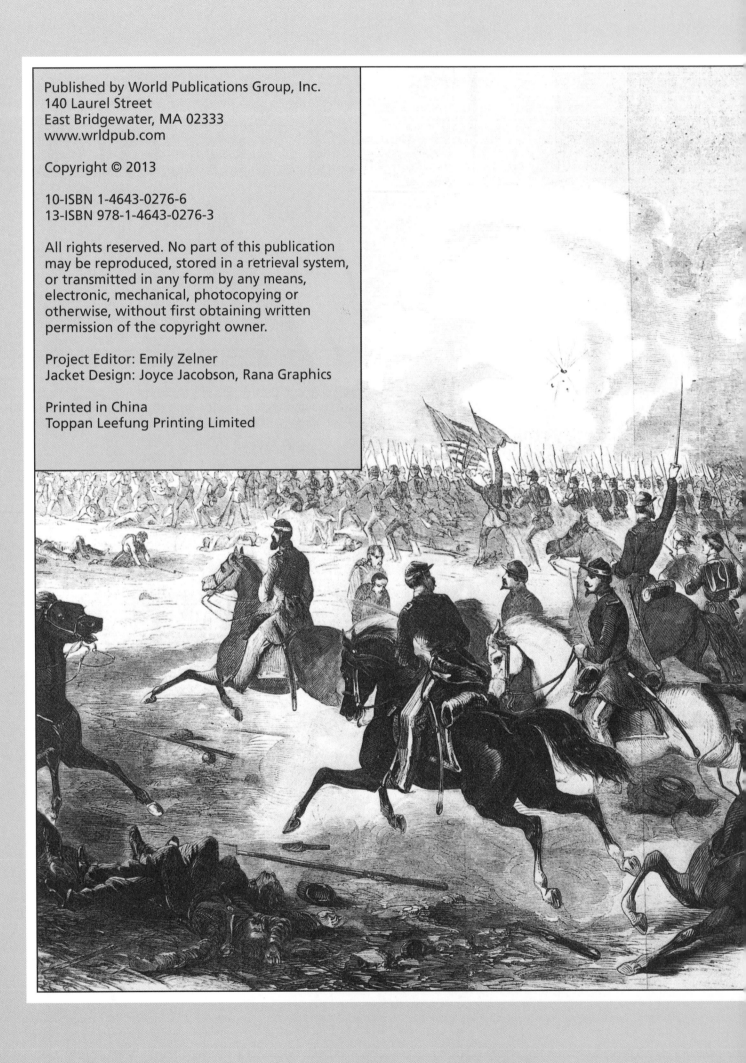

Published by World Publications Group, Inc.
140 Laurel Street
East Bridgewater, MA 02333
www.wrldpub.com

Copyright © 2013

10-ISBN 1-4643-0276-6
13-ISBN 978-1-4643-0276-3

Project Editor: Emily Zelner
Jacket Design: Joyce Jacobson, Rana Graphics

Printed in China
Toppan Leefung Printing Limited

CONTENTS

FOREWORD

The 16th President of the United States was the humblest in his origins and the greatest in his growth. The terrible trauma of the nation, the American Civil War, called forth profound powers of thought and will in this man. But the miracle would never have occurred if Lincoln had not already developed an acute awareness of destiny's demands. Here is how he himself put the case in his Second Annual Message of December 1, 1862:

'Fellow-citizens, we cannot escape history. We of this Congress and this administration will be remembered in spite of ourselves. No personal significance, or insignificance, can spare one or another of us. The fiery trial through which we pass will light us down, in honor or dishonor, to the latest generation.'

And so it was. The poet Walt Whitman described Lincoln as being quite 'the grandest figure on the crowded canvas of the drama of the nineteenth century.' On the floor of the House of Representatives in 1923 Congressman Homer Koch of Kansas spoke no less than the truth in the poetic tribute:

There is no new thing to be said about Lincoln. There is no new thing to be said of the mountains, or of the sea, or of the stars. The years go their way, but the same old mountains lift their granite shoulders above the drifting clouds; the same mysterious sea beats upon the shore, the same silent stars keep holy vigil above a tired world. But to the mountains and sea and stars men turn forever in unwearied homage. And thus with Lincoln. For he was a mountain in grandeur of soul, he was a sea in deep undervoice of mystic loneliness, he was a star in steadfast purity of purpose and service. And he abides.

Lincoln had received less than a full year of formal schooling in his whole life. His initial and purely local renown had been in the realms of axe-wielding, joking and scuffling. His early career on the frontier was halting, hardscrabble and debt-ridden. His middle years as a self-taught circuit-riding country lawyer and minor politician were respectable but obscure. Furthermore, he was plagued with serious bouts of depression throughout his life. His only friends and helpers were people whom he himself managed to draw around him over the years. The potent, moneyed aristocracy of the eastern States regarded Lincoln, almost until the end, as a gawky bumpkin. How did this man — this emotionally divided and paradoxical man — come to such greatness at last?

Over one hundred years after his death, Abraham Lincoln is still one of our best-known Presidents. His familiarity may be due in part to the number of photographs that survive, such as this one taken by Mathew Brady in January 1864.

THE
BACKWOODS
BOY

Some people maintain that heredity is the making of individual men and women. Others look to environment and upbringing for clues to a person's later career. In Lincoln's case, however, neither his genetic inheritance nor the surroundings of his childhood and youth offer the least foreshadowing of President Lincoln in his prime.

Abraham Lincoln's father, Thomas, was orphaned at the age of six when Indians raided his family's just-cleared Kentucky farm. While previous generations of pioneering Lincolns had done fairly well in Massachusetts, Pennsylvania, and Virginia, Thomas was fated to a hard and laboring life on the frontier. He possessed the same coarse black hair and leathery complexion as his son, but in almost every other respect they were opposites. The stocky and illiterate carpenter and farmer must have felt baffled by his gangling, sensitive, bookish son.

Lincoln's mother was of even humbler origin: a wiry, prematurely-wrinkled frontierswoman suffering from 'want of teeth.' Nancy Hanks was born out of wedlock to an obscure mountain girl named Lucy Hanks — who later married one Henry Sparrow and settled down on a Kentucky farm — and an unknown father. Lincoln seems to have believed that his maternal grandfather was a Virginia aristocrat who had either proved

heartless or met a tragic fate. That would be a natural thing for his mother to tell him, and for the boy to accept. However, a significant fraction of Lincoln's geneological heritage will never be accounted for.

Some political foes tried to tarbrush him in their time with sneering references to 'the Liberian Lincolns' and 'the Ethiope tribe of Hanks.' The inference, so damning then, has a certain appeal in our less racist day. There is also a faint possibility that Abe's maternal grandfather was Indian. Abe's aquiline features, his spare yet wiry physique, and his moccasin-soft way of walking might point in that direction.

Thomas Lincoln and Nancy Hanks were married on June 12, 1806, near Beechland, Washington County, Kentucky. They built a log cabin at Elizabethtown in Hardin County. Their first child, Sarah, was born the following year. In 1808 the Lincolns bought a farm at 'Sinking Spring' nearby and built another one-room log cabin there. The single door swung on leather hinges. The one small window overlooked rolling meadows, low hills and a river which formed a lake at the foot of the Lincoln property.

It was here that Abraham Lincoln was born on February 12, 1809. Only six years before, President Thomas Jefferson had purchased what was then called 'Louisiana' from Napoleon of France for some $27

The Gettysburg Address

Abraham Lincoln

Fourscore and seven years ago our fathers brought forth, on this continent, a new nation, conceived in liberty, and dedicated to the proposition that all men are created equal.

Now we are engaged in a great civil war, testing whether that nation, or any nation so conceived, and so dedicated, can long endure. We are met on a great battle-field of that war. We have come to dedicate a portion of that field, as a final resting-place for those who here gave their lives, that that nation might live. It is altogether fitting and proper that we should do this.

But, in a larger sense, we cannot dedicate, we cannot consecrate—we cannot hallow—this ground. The brave men, living and dead, who struggled here, have consecrated it far above our poor power to add or detract. The world will little note, nor long remember what we say here, but it can never forget what they did here. It is for us the living, rather, to be dedicated here to the unfinished work which they who fought here have thus far so nobly advanced. It is rather for us to be here dedicated to the great task remaining before us—that from these honored dead we take increased devotion to that cause for which they here gave the last full measure of devotion—that we here highly resolve that these dead shall not have died in vain— that this nation, under God, shall have a new birth of freedom, and that government of the people, by the people, for the people, shall not perish from the earth.

— President Lincoln delivered the Gettysburg Address on November 19, 1863, on the battlefield near Gettysburg, Pennsylvania.

million or about four cents per acre. Excluding only the Texas-New Mexico area (still in Spanish possession) this territory centered on the Mississippi basin and extended all the way west to the Rocky Mountains. Settlers not unlike the Lincolns were starting to wrest its million square miles from the Indians. The broad, bare foundations of America's material greatness would be laid down in Lincoln's own lifetime.

Thomas Lincoln was a restless man with a perverse instinct for bad bargains in land. When Abraham was three the family moved again, to start a farm beside the old Cumberland Trail at Knob Creek, Kentucky. A one-room schoolhouse stood only two miles away. The Lincoln children occasionally walked over to learn their ABCs. But it was not long before a property dispute drove Thomas on. Impatiently, on a raw day in December 1816, the Lincolns packed their few personal possessions on horseback and set out to the northwest for the Ohio River.

Crossing by ferry, they plunged on into the thickly forested Indiana wilderness. Sometimes Thomas had to go ahead to hack a path through the dense underbrush for the horses to follow. Sixteen miles north of the river, they halted on a knoll, and constructed a lean-to made of logs and boughs, with nothing but a roaring fire to protect its open south side from the

Previous spread: For many poor or ne'er-do-well farmers like Thomas Lincoln, the wealth of game and the availability of new land were incentives to settling the frontier.

Left: By 1800 the log cabin, brought to the New World by the Swedish settlers of Delaware, was a familiar sight throughout the frontier territories.
Above: Logs were easily adapted to fence rails, but clearing the land was back-breaking labor.

winter blast. They had some store of food, and snow provided their water, but the months which they spent holed-up must have been hard indeed.

Not until springtime were the Lincolns able to build the windowless, dirt-floored cabin which was to be their new home. At first the family subsisted on venison and wildfowl as well as wild honey, berries and other fruits in season. Lincoln himself shot a wild turkey at the age of eight, but hunting distressed him. Never after that would he 'pull a trigger on any larger game.'

Lincoln described this time in a third-person autobiographical sketch in 1860: 'The clearing away of surplus wood was the great task ahead. Abraham, though still very young, was large for his age, and had an axe put into his hands at once; and from that till within his twenty-third year, he was almost constantly handling that most useful instrument — less, of course, in plowing and harvesting seasons.'

The Lincolns were soon joined by a Hanks aunt and

Left: *Sarah Bush Johnston married Thomas Lincoln in 1819. A widow from Kentucky, she encouraged her step-son to study and to read. Thomas Lincoln had no understanding of his son's thirst for knowledge.*

Above: *Flatboats were frequently used for transportation of people and goods along the rivers. They could be built in any size in a matter of days, and sold for timber at the end of the voyage.*

uncle, plus an illegitimate child named Dennis Hanks, who soon became Lincoln's best friend. In the late summer of 1818, an epidemic known to the pioneers simply as milksick swept across southwestern Indiana. Lincoln's mother, aunt, and uncle all succumbed. Thomas Lincoln built the coffins, and dug the graves not far from his homestead door. No minister was to be found so Thomas himself conducted the burial service as best he could from memory.

That winter must have represented a dreadful nadir in the lives of Thomas Lincoln, Dennis Hanks, twelve-year-old Sarah and nine-year-old Abraham. The four lived huddled together on the edge of nowhere, in the harsh wilderness. Something of this comes through in a verse which Lincoln composed some 20 years afterward:

> When first my father settled here,
> 'Twas then the frontier line:
> The panther's scream filled night with fear
> And bears preyed on the swine.

One of Lincoln's chores was to carry grist from the small farm to a neighbor's mill. He himself used to drive the old millhorse around its circular track to turn the millstone and grind the grist to flour. 'Git up,' the

lad called out one day, plying the horsewhip — and the mare rebelled. It kicked out suddenly, knocking him flat. Lincoln was carried home and put to bed in the cabin. When he returned to consciousness next morning, legend insists, he sat up in bed and finished his command to the absent mare: 'Git up, you old hussy!'

The following winter, Thomas journeyed back to Elizabethtown, Kentucky, to find a second wife in the widow Sarah Bush Johnston, who had three growing children of her own. Loading Sarah together with her family and household goods on to a borrowed wagon drawn by a four-horse team, he returned home in triumph. With nine people now crowded into the one-room cabin, another kind of life overtook Lincoln. It must have been more cheerful, yet cramping too.

His fond, energetic stepmother — 'my angel mother' as he recalled her — saw to it that Lincoln received a few more precious weeks of schooling from itinerant teachers. She also seems to have brought an arithmetic schoolbook with her to Indiana, and Lincoln worried through that on his own. In old age his stepmother proudly recalled how he used to work out sums in charcoal upon a slab of wood, whittling each one down in turn to clear the board for the next problem. Later on he received a 'sum book' of blank pages, from which this earliest known scrap of his writing has been preserved:

> Abraham Lincoln, his hand and pen,
> He will be good, but God knows when.

Books were pure and necessary nourishment to the boy. The few that he could borrow or otherwise obtain,

Lincoln's birthplace in Hardin County, Kentucky, is now a National Shrine, but the cabin was in a state of utter dilapidation when this photograph was taken in the nineteenth century. The method of cabin construction is easily understood, and on the right the ends of the beams supporting the second floor can be seen. This loft would have been reached by a crude ladder. The panes of glass in the single window were a great luxury on the frontier, where window frames were more often filled with translucent hide.

15

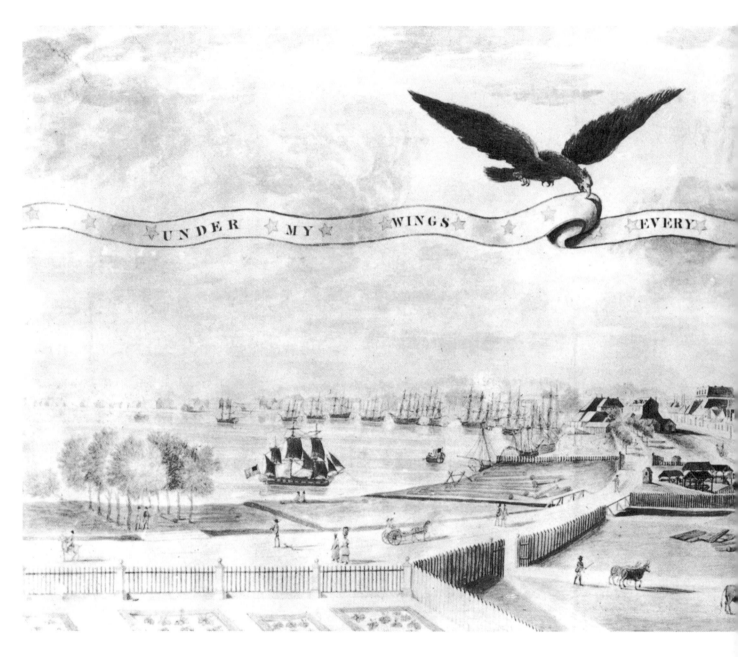

UNDER ⋆ MY ⋆ WINGS⋆ EVERY

The city of New Orleans, founded in 1718 by French settlers, had become a part of the United States as recently as 1803, following the Louisiana Purchase. A city which cherished its French and Spanish heritage, New Orleans was the largest and most exotic metropolis Lincoln had ever seen, when he and Allen Gentry brought a flatboat down the Mississippi in 1828.

Lincoln digested thoroughly. When plowing, it was said, Lincoln used to 'rest the horses' at the end of each furrow while he perused a page or two.

Reading Parson Weems's *Life of Washington*, he was struck by the sufferings of the soldiers at Valley Forge. 'There must have been something more than common that these men struggled for,' he concluded.

Aesop's Fables, Robinson Crusoe, Pilgrim's Progress and Grimshaw's *History of the United States* seem to have appealed to him more than the family Bible. Yet that book, above all, helped to shape the style of Lincoln's own prodigious (although slowly and pain-

fully born) literary genius.

In March of 1820, when Lincoln was 11, a most important piece of legislation for the nation's future came into being. This was the so-called Missouri Compromise which disallowed slave-holding in the northern section of what was still called Louisiana Purchase territory. The Lincolns and their friends were anti-slavery in any case, not only for moral reasons but also because they felt that the frontier rightly belonged to their own sort. By this they meant poor white settlers as opposed to slave-holding plantation owners.

Meanwhile, Indiana was filling rapidly. A man named James Gentry, who had arrived about the same time that the Lincolns did, parlayed his thousand-acre holding into the village of Gentryville, a mile and a half from the Lincoln homestead. Dennis Hanks later recalled that when the day's chores were done he and Lincoln would go over to Gentryville's general store.

the nearby Pigeon Creek Baptist church, which Lincoln too must have attended, and yet he never joined. This too set him apart from his peers. And finally, so did his sobriety. Corn whiskey at pennies per potful was the standard comfort and solace of frontier society — not excepting the Lincoln household — yet Abraham Lincoln would remain a water-drinker all his life.

Doubtless the common thread linking these special traits was the future President's growing sense that he was a peculiar person — singled out by his own size, strength, wit and force of feeling — who must for that very reason exercise constant self-control. The intolerant, fire-and-brimstone emotionalism of frontier religion, for example, would represent a perceived threat to Lincoln's inner equilibrium — as would blasphemous language, sexual license of any sort, and alcohol.

Farming and clearing land, both on the family property and as a hired hand, occupied Lincoln's teenage years. When he was 17 his sister Sarah married and went away (she was to die in childbirth not long afterward). At 19, Lincoln joined forces with Allen Gentry — of the neighboring Gentryville Gentrys — to undertake a thousand-mile journey down along the Father of Waters all the way to New Orleans.

They built their own flatboat for the purpose, hewing its planks from riverside oaks which they had felled themselves, and loading it with produce from the Gentry farm. The wide wandering water took them on its back. By day they would float and pole along; by night they tied up at trees along the Mississippi riverbank. Below Baton Rouge on the so-called Sugar Coast one night, seven men crept aboard as the boys slept. Lincoln wakened, reached for his crab-apple club, and leaped up swinging. He was struck on the head, yet hardly noticed the blow. Allen also fought like a cornered wildcat, and soon the attackers fled. Until he reached New Orleans Lincoln wore a bandana headdress tilted rakishly to cover the gash over his right eye. This incident left a permanent scar upon his brow.

From Lincoln's perspective, how did the city seem? He and his partner, hayseeds both, must have been overwhelmed by New Orleans, the most cosmopolitan and the largest city either of them had ever seen, a remarkable potpourri of colourful throngs, cobblestone streets, wrought-iron balustrades, creole culture, gambling halls, pillared mansions, rude hovels, teeming slave-markets, French wine bars and Jamaica rum dens. They sold their boat along with its cargo, and returned upriver by steamer. Lincoln's wages for the three-month adventure: $24. Whatever remained of this amount he turned over to his father. Custom, and the law, required as much of all sons under 21.

Soon he would find himself free to seek his own fortune, but not quite yet. Besides, Lincoln never was in a hurry. He had much to ponder, and much already to digest.

There they would sit around the crackerbarrel or the stove to swap yarns and yearnings with other farm boys. As the evening wore on Dennis would 'cuss Abe most heartily' for staying so late.

Plainly, the future lawyer and politician loved company, and he already revelled in verbal play. Yet there were many things about the boy, besides his bookishness, which set Lincoln apart from his peers. Tall for his age, he was also extremely strong. Lincoln used to demonstrate this by gripping a heavy axe at the end of its handle and holding it at arm's length parallel to the ground. Although he delighted in horseplay and coarse jokes, he refrained from swearing. Moreover, young Abraham was regarded as personally chaste if not actually embarrassed by female company. 'A woman is the only thing I am afraid of,' he once confessed with a smile, 'that I know can't hurt me.'

Lincoln's father and stepmother both belonged to

THE HARDSCRABBLER

In February 1830, Thomas Lincoln uprooted his family yet again. Over in Illinois, he had heard, there was flat, black-soil prairie for the taking. There, the old man felt sure, he could toil less and prosper more. Abraham Lincoln tended to worry things through in slow deliberate style, but his father seemed just the opposite. Once more Thomas Lincoln was moving along with the human tide which would soon span the continent.

The Indiana farm sold for $125. The family traveled westward in three wagons, one drawn by a four-horse team, and the others by oxen. Abe, who had just come of age, drove one of the ox-teams. Their 200-mile journey through snowy semi-wilderness fretted with icy streams ended a few miles west of Decatur, on the north bank of the Sangamon River, where the forest met the boundless prairie. There the Lincolns built a cabin. That spring they cleared 15 acres of ground. And during the summer Lincoln hired himself out to split no less than 4000 fence-rails for neighboring farmers.

With the coming of autumn, almost the whole family contracted unexplained chills and fevers. In December, a blizzard introduced what was to be celebrated in song and story as Illinois' 'Winter of the Deep Snow.' For nine weeks, nothing but wolves and swirling snow moved freely round the farm. Below-zero temperatures prevailed. The spring thaw came at last, bringing disastrous floods in its wake. Thomas Lincoln resolved to move again, to nearby Coles County. But this time Lincoln bestirred himself to get away, to strike out on his own in a direction other than pioneer homesteading.

Although an 'uneducated, friendless and penniless boy,' as he described himself, Lincoln could read, write, 'cipher,' and above all he could think. Perhaps the world might find use for his head, not just his hands. In any case, he'd grown determined to find out. He would hardly ever see his restless father again.

Lincoln's stepbrother John Johnston and cousin John Hanks set off with him, descending the Sangamon

Lincoln, like many Americans raised in the backwoods, was a master axman. The experience of using an ax continuously from childhood gave him the proficiency and accuracy necessary to split rails.

River by canoe. They disembarked at Judy's Ferry, where the village of Riverton now stands. From there they walked four miles to a growing settlement of smoke-plumed cabins in a magnificent grove on the prairie. This was Springfield, Illinois, the setting for much of Lincoln's subsequent career. In Andrew Elliott's Buckhorn Tavern on the town square, the young men found the man they were looking for: a fast-talking entrepreneur named Denton Offutt, who had once promised Lincoln a job.

Yes, Offutt said, if the boys would build him an 80-foot flatboat, load it with the corn, barreled pork and live swine which he meant to purchase, pole it on down to distant New Orleans, sell the produce there for him, and return by paddle-wheeler, he'd pay them each $12 a month for their trouble.

On their return from New Orleans, Offutt gave Lincoln a job as resident manager of a store and gristmill at New Salem, a hamlet on the banks of the Sangamon River 20 miles below Springfield.

Starting in July 1831, Lincoln spent six years at New Salem. The village boasted a tavern, two saloons, two stores, two doctors, a blacksmith, a cooper, a cobbler, a hatter and a wheelwright. It contained an unruly element known as the Clary's Grove Boys, but took pride in its local 'intellectuals' as well. Among the latter were schoolmaster Mentor Graham, magistrate Bowling Green, and a Dartmouth graduate named Dr. John Allen who had come west to improve his health. There was also an eccentric named Jack Kelso, a shambling Scotsman far from his native land, who lived by hunting and fishing. In company with these people, Lincoln found real intellectual challenge for the first time in his life.

For one thing, Mentor Graham lent Lincoln books such as Edward Gibbons' *Decline and Fall of the Roman Empire* and Thomas Paine's *The Age of Reason*, thus vastly expanding his intellectual horizons. For another, Bowling Green encouraged Abe to try his hand at writing out deeds and contracts, and even to plead a few cases informally at Green's own hearings. Finally, John Allen's 'New Salem Debating Society' welcomed Lincoln and was in turn pleasantly surprised by him. As he rose to speak there for the first time, another member recalled:

> *A perceptible smile at once lit up the faces of the audience, for all anticipated the relation of some humorous story, but he opened up the discussion in splendid style, to the infinite astonishment of his friends. As he warmed to his subject, his hands would forsake their pockets, and would enforce his ideas by awkward gestures; but would very soon seek their resting-place. He pursued the question with reason and argument so pithy that all were amazed. The president, at his fireside after the meeting, remarked to his wife that there was more than wit and fun in Abe's head; that he was already a fine speaker; that all he lacked was culture.*

The ragged eccentric Jack Kelso gave Lincoln a deeper kind of culture than the town worthies could. Kelso could quote whole reams of Shakespeare and Robert Burns. Between tugs at his fishing line, or pulls at his little brown jug, the Scottish recluse would recite what he knew while Lincoln listened attentively.

When Jack Armstrong, leader of the Clary Grove Boys, boisterously offered to wrestle Lincoln in a challenge match, there was no escaping the contest.

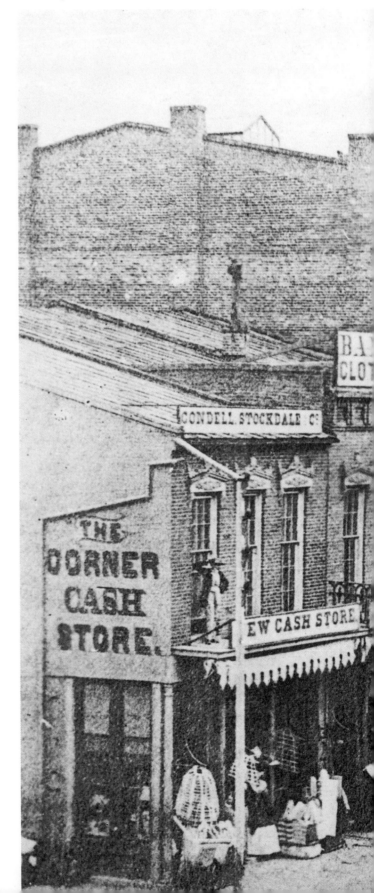

Heavy bets were made, with Offutt putting the most money on his man. The whole town turned out for the sport. Lincoln proved to be all muscle, far stronger than he looked. After half an hour's hard grappling, Lincoln had Armstrong very nearly pinned. When the rest of the gang swarmed out to rescue their sweating hero, Lincoln sprang up. Setting his back against a wall, he fiercely dared the whole lot to fight him — one at a time.

Springfield, Illinois, in the 1840s was typical of the growing towns in the New Republic, with formal brick stores facing an unpaved street and a raised sidewalk.

The crisis was resolved when Armstrong himself slouched forward to shake hands and declare the contest a draw. Lincoln was cheerfully enrolled as an honorary member of the Clary Grovers. His autobiographical sketch of 1860 summarizes what happened after that:

In less than a year Offutt's business was failing — had almost failed — when the Black Hawk War of 1832 broke out. Abraham joined a volunteer company, and, to his own surprise, was elected captain of it. He says he has not since had any success in life which gave him so much satisfaction. He went to the campaign, served near three months, met the ordinary hardships of such an expedition, but was in no battle....

Chief Black Hawk's war party of 500 Sauk and Fox braves had some success in northern Illinois at first. At one point, Lincoln discovered and helped to bury five white men killed in a skirmish. 'The red light of the morning sun,' he wrote, 'was streaming upon them as they lay heads towards us on the ground. And every man had a round red spot on top of his head, about as big as a dollar where the redskins had

taken his scalp... and the red sunlight seemed to paint everything all over. I remember that one man had on buckskin breeches.'

The laconic and yet painterly vividness of that description reveals yet another aspect of the man. For all his sober ruggedness of thought, Lincoln had a touch of the poet in him as well. He was 'mystically inclined' as he himself once confessed in a letter to a friend. After his death, his widow was to say that Lincoln had been a truly religious person but his religion was 'a kind of poetry in his nature.'

Returning from the campaign, and encouraged by his great popularity among his immediate neighbors, he the same year ran for the legislature, and was beaten — his own precinct, however, casting its votes 227 for and 7 against him.... This was the only time Abraham was ever beaten on a direct vote of the people.

He was now without means and out of business but was anxious to remain with his friends who had treated him with so much generosity, especially as he had nothing elsewhere to go to. He studied what he should do — thought of learning the blacksmith trade — thought of trying to study law — rather thought he could not succeed

Top left: *The volunteer company that Lincoln captained in the Black Hawk War was typical of the militia that would be raised to defend settlements against Indian attack — inexperienced in military matters, but remarkable sharpshooters.*

Above: *The Black Hawk War was one of many Indian risings, which took place as the western movement brought more settlers into tribal lands.*

Left: *Black Hawk, Chief of the Sauk tribe, was defeated in August 1832.*

at that without a better education. Before long, strangely enough, a man offered to sell, and did sell, to Abraham and another as poor as himself, an old stock of goods upon credit. They opened as merchants, and ... did nothing but get deeper and deeper in debt. He was appointed postmaster at New Salem — the post being too insignificant to make his politics an objection. The store winked out. The surveyor of Sangamon offered to depute to Abraham that portion of his work which was within his part of the county. He accepted, procured a compass and chain, studied Flint and Gibson a little, and went at it. This procured bread, and kept soul and body together. The election of 1834 came, and he was then elected to the legislature by the highest vote cast for any candidate.

One thing for which he had no talent at all was business. When Offutt left New Salem to develop business interests elsewhere, Lincoln remained to flounder. His instinct for buying the wrong commercial properties recalls his father's penchant for settling on unlikely real estate. He chose an alcoholic for a business partner, while he read, wandered, schemed and dreamed when he ought to have been minding the store. His partner soon died, leaving Lincoln their mutual debt of $1100 — a perfectly enormous sum at that time and place.

Instead of leaving town as many a less scrupulous man would have done, the bankrupt simply swore to pay every penny back over the years; and pay it he eventually would — thus earning the sobriquet 'Honest Abe.' Meanwhile he took whatever work his friends and neighbors found to throw his way.

Finally, however, foreclosure was inevitable and his personal effects were disposed of at auction. Well-wishers bought his horse and his surveying tools on that occasion; otherwise Lincoln would have found himself with nothing — except for a single treasure which nobody else wanted. This was Blackstone's *Commentaries*, the classic lawbook of its day. Lincoln had discovered the volume at the bottom of a barrel of junk which he'd purchased 'to help a fellow out' while still a storekeeper. There did seem to be destiny in such an event, fuel for Abe's growing philosophical conviction that, as he put it, 'the human mind is impelled to action or held in rest by some power over which the mind has no control.'

For months he pored over Blackstone's book; he took the whole thing, like a dear friend, home into his head. Blackstone was Lincoln's true professor, his main school of law.

Campaigning for a seat on the state legislature in 1834, Lincoln offered no public pronouncements, let alone promises. He simply dropped by for chats with all the friends he'd made as village postmaster, part-time land-surveyor, and occasional hired hand. It is said that 30 farmers promised him their vote after he'd bested the lot in an impromptu wheat-cradling contest. His stoical and humorous good fellowship won the day. Abraham Lincoln was only 25 when his Sangamon County constituents saw him off to the state capital — Vandalia.

Around Vandalia's muddy public square with its statehouse of crumbling brick clustered a few taverns, inns, stables and cabins for a population of about 800. Lincoln put up at the tavern favored by other legislators in his own Whig party. He wore a tailored suit now for the first time in his life: a $60, rumpled but respectable affair, bought on credit.

His legislative labors must have seemed a kind of game to him, if not actual imposture, at first. But Lincoln soon saw that most of his colleagues were very nearly as young and inexperienced as himself. Moreover, the Whig platform which he diligently

labored to implement was straight forward enough in its opposition to the Democratic one.

The Democrats at Vandalia had a fiery young leader in Stephen A. Douglas, who was destined to be Lincoln's great public rival. Democrats stood against the banks and against too much government control.

The Whigs, for their part, were led by a young Springfield attorney named John Todd Stuart. They demanded more roads, railroads and waterways for Illinois, all financed through state banks, plus ultimate removal of the capital itself from sleepy Vandalia north to Stuart's native Springfield.

Lincoln soon proved himself to be a talented bill-

drafter and a popular deputy floor leader. To Stuart, he confessed his old dream of becoming a lawyer. 'Why not?' was Stuart's response. In Illinois one needed no law degree, and the state bar examination was little more than a formality.

When the legislative session ended in February 1835, Lincoln received $258 for his labors. Then he and Stuart traveled north together as far as Springfield, where Lincoln borrowed a few law books to take on home to New Salem. Among them: Chitty's *Pleadings* and Story's *Equity*.

A piece of advice which Lincoln gave to a young friend in later years clarifies his own studies of 1835.

Vandalia was the capital of the state of Illinois until 1837, when the government and courts moved to the more centrally located city of Springfield.

'If you are resolutely determined to make a lawyer of yourself,' he explained, 'the thing is more than half done already. It is but a small matter whether you read with anybody or not. I did not read with anyone. Get the books, and read and study them till you understand them in their principal features; and that is the main thing. It is of no consequence to be in a large town... The books, and your capacity for understanding them, are just the same in all places.'

That summer, a pretty local girl named Anne

Rutledge died of a fever at New Salem. Lincoln knew her well, for he had once roomed above her father's tavern. Her death plunged him into weeks of severe depression — or 'hypochondria' as it was known at the time. He continued to sink into a sometimes desperately melancholic condition at intervals throughout the rest of life.

Was Lincoln passionately in love with Anne Rutledge? Did her untimely death darken his whole existence forever afterward? The answer to the first question may well be positive, although we possess not a shred of actual evidence to that effect. However — numerous romancers to the contrary — the answer to the second question is probably negative. Lincoln was no slender reed, and he would face far worse things than Anne Rutledge's death without breaking.

In cold fact, Lincoln soon emerged from his period of grief to dance attendance upon a New Salem visitor named Mary Owens. She was plainly in search of a husband. He, however, struck the lady as 'deficient in those little links which make up the chain of a woman's happiness.' And yet despite strong reservations on both sides they did become engaged. In a letter written some time afterwards Lincoln laughed off the whole business:

> *I knew she was over-size, but now she appeared a fair match for Falstaff. I knew she was called an 'old maid,' and I felt no doubt of the truth of at least half the appellation, but now, when I beheld her, I could not for my life avoid thinking of my mother; and this, not from withered features — for her skin was too full of fat to permit its contracting into wrinkles — but from her want of teeth, weatherbeaten appearance in general, and from a kind of notion that ran in my head that nothing could have commenced at the size of infancy and reached her present bulk in less than thirty-five or forty years; and, in short, I was not at all pleased with her. But what could I do?... Others have been made fools of by the girls, but this can never in truth be said of me. I most emphatically, in this instance, made a fool of myself. I have now come to the conclusion never again to think of marrying, and for this reason — I can never be satisfied with anyone who would be blockhead enough to have me.'*

Lincoln told funny stories to combat depression. He could be cutting, but then too he had a most endearing way of turning wit's edge against himself. But the astonishing thing which this account demonstrates is the early flowering and extreme versatility of Lincoln's literary genius. He was to become a forcefully affecting letter-writer, a truly superb orator and a resonant prose-poet. Meanwhile, Lincoln had already parlayed his rudimentary knowledge into stylistic mastery. The subtle, dry cadence of Lincoln's casual composition brings to mind no less a humorist than Mark Twain.

Politically, and professionally too, Lincoln was almost out of the woods. Returned to the state legislature by an overwhelming vote, he lobbied adroitly for

the removal of the whole body to Springfield. On February 28, 1837, this Whig proposal gained adoption. Then on the first of March the Supreme Court of Illinois granted Abraham Lincoln a certificate of admission to the bar. Subsequently the Whig floor leader John T. Stuart invited Lincoln to be his partner in private law practice at Springfield. The legislature adjourned on March 15. Lincoln returned to New Salem, but only to bid his friends a fond farewell. He was moving permanently to the new capital.

Springfield was then a fairly raw frontier town of some 2000 people. Hogs snuffled in the mud and dust of the streets. Hymn-singing at the six churches counterpointed the thumps and shouts emanating from more than twice that number of saloons. Sudden storms would flood the backyard privies. Prairie fires sometimes lit the horizon at night, raining ashes upon the pious and the naughty too. The carriages of the new rich splattered pedestrian shoppers who scuttled on plank walks from store to store. White clapboard mansions alternated with hovels of log and sod.

As the village of New Salem had been to tiny Gentryville, so Springfield was to New Salem from Lincoln's point of view.

THE MAN IN THE STOVEPIPE HAT

On April 15, 1837, Abraham Lincoln rode into Springfield on a borrowed horse. All his earthly goods were in his saddlebags. He was just 28 years old, and he had 28 more years — to the day — of life still ahead.

A storekeeper named Joshua Speed noticed Lincoln's arrival and remarked that he 'never saw so gloomy and melancholy a face in my life.' Lincoln was going into battle for advancement in a greater world than he had yet known; a rough arena thronged with proud and ruthless men. He must have doubted his chances of success.

Speed was a husky young Kentuckian whose abolitionist leanings had caused him to drop out of college and come north. Touched by Lincoln's melancholy at first meeting, he found himself enchanted when the warm Lincoln wit broke through. On impulse he invited Lincoln to share his double bed in the room over the store. 'Well, Speed, I'm moved,' Lincoln replied with a grin, dumping his saddlebags on the floor. The pair would room together for the following four years.

Both tended to be ill-at-ease with women, and both liked nothing better than relaxing in male company. Around the great hearth at the back of Speed's store they held bawdy, boisterous bull-sessions with other rising merchants, lawyers and politicians. There Lincoln honed his already keen dialectical skills, and stocked up on the humorous anecdotes which would become part of his stock-in-trade.

Right: *The fashionable high hat of the mid-nineteenth century only served to accentuate Lincoln's height. It made him an easy figure to caricature, but it also gave him a dignity the soft hat worn by Allan Pinkerton (left) would have lessened.*

Meanwhile the Stuart-Lincoln law partnership prospered, and so did their political alliance. When Stuart was elected to Congress, Lincoln kept him informed on the home front. Typical of their friendship is a note from Lincoln to Stuart in Washington, dated March 1, 1840:

I have never seen the prospects of our party so bright in these parts as they are now. We shall carry this county by a larger majority than we did in 1836... Yesterday [Stephen A.] Douglas, having chosen to consider himself insulted by something in the Journal, *undertook to cane [the editor, Simeon] Francis in the street. Francis caught him by the hair and jammed him back against a market-cart, where the matter ended with Francis being pulled away from him. The whole affair was so ludicrous that Francis and everybody else (Douglas excepted) have been laughing about it ever since.*

Political and journalistic tactics at that time were rough and ready, as that episode indicates. Editor Simeon Francis's pro-Whig *Sangamon Journal* of May 8, 1840, for instance, excoriates a rival newspaper for pretending that Lincoln haled 'from outward appearance originally from Liberia.' This 'unkindest cut of all,' Francis cheerfully concluded, 'comes with a bad grace from a member of the party whose very head and leader this same Mr. L. clearly showed in his speech to be clothed with the sable furs of Guinea — whose breath smells rank with devotion to the cause of Africa's sons — and whose very trail might be followed by scattered bunches of Nigger wool.'

In fact Lincoln had been stumping the state for William Henry Harrison, the Whig Presidential candidate, and attacking the Democratic nominee Martin Van Buren in any way he could. 'I know,' he declared, 'that the great volcano at Washington, roused and directed by the evil spirit that reigns there, is belching forth the lava of political corruption in a current broad and deep, which is sweeping with frightful velocity over the whole length and breadth of the land!'

Lincoln had gone on to point out that Van Buren once cast a vote for black suffrage in New York State — in those days an explosive charge to make.

Abolitionists already had achieved some strength in New York and more in New England. On the frontier, however, they were publicly scorned and secretly feared as inciters to violence. Meanwhile the slave-holding states of the South put prices on abolitionists' heads, 'dead or alive,' and lynched the few that they could reach.

Left: *By 1846, Abraham Lincoln was a rising young lawyer with political ambitions, about to serve in the House of Representatives. It was time to have a daguerreotype made for posterity. This is the earliest known likeness of Lincoln.*

Lincoln's own position on the slave question will always be a matter of debate among those who forget or choose to overlook the facts of political existence in a democracy. Under that system of government a country cannot be coerced into any major shift of direction — whether for evil or for good. The stability of the Union and the freedom of the people depend upon the voting citizen: a person who follows freely but refused to be forced. Therefore, the most effective leaders, such as Lincoln eventually became, do not march too far ahead of public opinion.

Lincoln regarded slavery as an unmitigated evil in itself, and a festering source of further evils to the commonwealth. He felt it must be checked, confined and done away with in the course of time. However, he further believed that this ought to be accomplished according to the will of the voters within the Union.

His fears for the safety of the Union itself were remarkably prescient, overriding all else. In his first important address (to the Young Men's Lyceum of Springfield) Lincoln argued:

As a nation of free men we must live for all time, or die by suicide. I hope I am over wary, but if I am not there is even now something of ill omen amongst us. I mean the increasing disregard for law which pervades the country — the growing disposition to substitute the wild and furious passions in lieu of the sober judgement of courts, and the worse than savage mobs for the executive ministers of justice.... Thus went on the process of hanging (in the South), from gamblers to Negroes, from Negroes to white citizens, and from these to strangers, till dead men were seen literally dangling from the boughs of trees upon every roadside, and in numbers almost sufficient to rival the native Spanish moss of the country as a drapery of the forest....

Whenever this effect shall be produced among us, whenever the vicious portion of the populace shall be permitted to gather in bands of hundreds and thousands, and burn churches, ravage and rob provision-stores, throw printing-presses into rivers, shoot editors, and hang and burn obnoxious persons at pleasure and with impunity, depend on it, this government cannot last. By such things the feelings of the best citizens will become more or less alienated from it, and thus it will be left without friends, or with too few, and those few too weak to make their friendship effectual. At such a time and under such circumstances, men of sufficient talent and ambition will not be wanting to seize the opportunity, strike the blow, and overturn that fair fabric which for the last half century has been the fondest hope of the lovers of freedom throughout the world.

The young lawyer in his tailored suit, and with a stovepipe hat considerably augmenting his six-foot four-inch presence, cast a noticeable shadow in Springfield. Local society tentatively began to welcome him. Thus Lincoln met Mary Anne Todd.

J.W.ORR N.Y.

Left: *The first blacks were brought into the original thirteen colonies in 1619 as indentured servants, but in 1664 Maryland passed a law mandating lifelong servitude for blacks. The other southern colonies followed suit with similar laws. Slave trading, though profitable, was never respectable and the horrors of the 'Middle Passage' began to attract the attention of more humane citizens. The slave trade was abolished in 1807, but the southern states continued to smuggle cargoes of 'black ivory'. The print (left) depicts the deck of* the slaver Wildfire, *which docked in Florida in April 1860.*

Above: *Slaveholders represented only a quarter of the white population of the South. It was only the great plantation owners (a mere one sixteenth) of that group who required cheap labor to plant and harvest their cash crops of tobacco, rice, indigo and cotton. Smaller landholders usually owned no more than six slaves.*

Following spread: *One of the ugliest aspects of slavery was* the slave market. *Although the importation of slaves was forbidden, traffic in slaves continued. A slave could never be sure that some economic reverse for his master would not result in his being sold, like a thoroughbred horse or any other asset. For the slave this might mean the break-up of his family. Sometimes the threat of such a sale was used to keep the slave in line. Being sold down the Mississippi River to one of the immense new cotton plantations of Mississippi or Alabama, was especially dreaded.*

Above: *The coastal plantations of the Carolinas raised indigo and rice. In the 1820s they suffered a series of hurricanes which flooded many of the fields with salt water. The plantation economy there never recovered, and many slaves were sold.*

Right: *In 1793 Eli Whitney developed a machine to separate cotton fibers from seed, a laborious process previously done by hand. This greatly increased the profitability of cotton, probably extending the existence of slavery, which had been in decline since the tobacco plantations of Virginia seemed to be worked out, unable to sustain a large number of slaves.*

At 21, Mary was living with a married sister and pleasantly engaging herself in the local social whirl — her sister was, after all, the daughter-in-law of the governor of Illinois. Brown-haired, blue-eyed, a trifle plump and rather short, she spiced her remarks with expressions in French learned at finishing school. In soft, genteel style she flaunted her aristocratic southern ancestry. She could be sweet or cuttingly sour, pliant or imperious, depending on her mood of the moment. Altogether, Mary seemed an unlikely bird-of-paradise to be attracted to the rustic Lincoln yet attracted she was and they were soon engaged.

What happened next is intriguing, even poignant, but unfortunately the subject of wildly conflicting accounts. All that is known for sure is that Lincoln broke off his engagement to Mary at the beginning of 1841, 'on the fatal first of January,' as he called it; and fell into a deathly depression thereafter. On January 23, he wrote to his partner Stuart in Washington:

For not giving you a general summary of news, you must pardon me; it is not in my power to do so. I am now the most miserable man living. If what I feel were equally distributed to the whole human family, there would not be one cheerful face on the earth. Whether I shall ever be better, I cannot tell; I awfully forbode I shall not. To remain as I am is impossible; I must die or be better, it appears to me.

Springfield gossiped that Lincoln had suffered 'two cat fits and a duck fit.' Mary herself confided to a friend that her former suitor 'deems me unworthy of notice, as I have not met him in the gay world for months... yet I would that the case were different, that he would once more resume his Station in society ... much, much happiness would it afford me.'

Joshua Speed had sold his store and set out for home in Louisville on the same 'fatal first of January' when Lincoln broke his engagement to Mary Todd. Lincoln had lost the two people dearest to him on the same day. Now he somewhat relieved his feelings in long letters to Speed.

In August 1841, Lincoln traveled to Louisville to complete his convalescence in the bosom of Speed's family. Speed returned the compliment by traveling back with Lincoln to Springfield for a protracted autumn visit. With Lincoln's encouragement, Speed himself took a wife in Kentucky early the following year.

Both men had felt themselves to be 'nervously

afflicted' and very likely incapable of marriage. Perhaps the bond between them was part of the trouble.

Lincoln was now meeting Mary again, but in secret, at the home of the *Journal* editor, Simeon Francis. The shy, psychologically bruised pair amused themselves by writing 'letters to the editor' which poked sharp fun at the Democratic State Auditor — a fighting Irishman named James Shields. These letters, signed 'Aunt Becca,' appeared in Francis's paper. They branded Shields 'a conceity dunce' and 'a liar as well as a fool.' The irrepressible 'Becca' added that if Shields wanted a fight, 'I never fights with any thing but broom-sticks or hot water or a shovel full of coals or some thing.'

Shields protested violently. Lincoln thereupon accepted responsibility for the letters. Mary's part in them was kept secret. A duel was soon arranged, with Lincoln to select the weapons. He chose cavalry sabres. The sometime railsplitter could no doubt have performed effectively with such a heavy length of sharp steel in hand. Whether for this reason or another, Shields finally elected to accept a semi-retraction in which Lincoln allowed that he had written as he did for political purposes, not out of any personal pique.

All this embarrassed Lincoln so acutely that he would never speak of it again. At the same time, it appears to have delighted Mary. Her gangling swain and secret friend had proved willing to fight a duel, in the 'gentlemanly' tradition of the south, purely to protect her good name! Well, then, her name would be his after all. Ladylike Mary Ann Todd, alias saucy Aunt Becca, secretly agreed to become Mrs. Lincoln.

On October 5, 1842, Lincoln wrote to ask his friend Speed: 'Are you now in *feeling* as well as in *judgement* glad you are married as you are?' Receiving an affirmative reply, he set the wedding day: November 4, 1842.

Mary kept her secret until the morning of the day itself. Her sister's family disapproved of Lincoln as being lower-class and unreliable. Besides, something might go wrong again. But when she was at last informed, Mary's sister instantly decreed that the wedding must take place that evening at their house, with an Episcopal service and a few hastily summoned friends in attendance.

Afterwards the happy although doubtless frightened couple — aged 33 and 23 respectively — drove by carriage through pelting rain to the Globe Tavern, where Lincoln had rented a room at $4 a week. This was to be their home for the next year. Their first son, Robert Todd, was born at the Globe.

Lincoln was still struggling to pay off 'the national debt,' as he called it, which he had long ago contracted as a dreamy young New Salem storekeeper. His law practice proved ever more remunerative, but it required him to ride far from home twice yearly, for three months at a stretch, attending circuit court. So Mary suffered much alone, in pinched circumstances such as she had never known, and which she regarded as degrading. Poverty is hell, she concluded. Unreasoning

Left: Mary Todd Lincoln (1819-1882), the daughter of a Kentucky planter, was staying with her sister in Springfield when she met Lincoln in 1849. After a broken engagement, they were married in 1842.

Lincoln's house in Springfield was built as a story-and-a-half cottage. In 1844 Lincoln paid $1200 for the house, where the three youngest children were born. It was later extended to two stories, and is still standing.

In the Sangamon Circuit court—
July term A.D. 1845—

Jonathan Miller &
Susan Miller
ads
William Beaty &
Martha Ann Beaty

Case, in Slander

And the said defendants come
and defend the wrong and injury, when, where
&c. and say ~~they are to~~ the said Susan is
not guilty, in manner and form as the said
plaintiffs, in their said declaration have alleged;
and of this, they, the said defendants, put themselves upon the country &c.

Lincoln & Herndon p.q

=2=
And for further plea in this behalf the said defendants (now disclaiming all intention of affirming the
truth of the supposed slanderous words in the said
declaration mentioned) say plaintiffs actio non, because they say that at time of the supposed speaking of the supposed slanderous words in the said
declaration mentioned, by the said Susan, she,
the said Susan did speak the said words, in the
connection following and not otherwise, that is
to say: "I" (the said Susan meaning) "have understood
that Mrs Beaty" (the said Martha Ann, meaning) "and
Dr Sulivan were seen together in Beaty's" (the said
Williams, meaning) "stable, one morning, very early, in
the very act—" "It certainly is a fact—" "Jo Shepherd
can prove it by two respectable witnesses," "Mrs Beaty" (the said Martha Ann meaning) "and Dr Sulivan
were seen in the very act—" "They" (the said Martha
Ann, and the said Dr Sulivan meaning) were caught

fear of it would haunt her from then on.

At last, in January 1844, Lincoln was able to lay-out $1200 for a modest frame house and lot — with trees, privies, and a stable — on the corner of Eighth and Jackson Streets not far from his office. His debts were now retired and his annual income was creeping up over the $1500 mark. His second son, Edward, was born in 1846.

Now Mary could afford a maid. It drove her mad that Lincoln would still answer the door and receive callers in his stocking feet instead of letting the maid do it. Another thing that galled her was his way of stretching out on the hall floor, resting his head upon the back of an uptilted chair, to read the newspapers aloud. Again, he was subject to periods of melancholy abstraction, during which he ignored his family. On the positive side, however, Lincoln loved romping with their little boys. Moreover, the Lincolns always protected and spoke well of each other. Throughout their marriage they remained loyal and tender. Friends and relations who believed that 'poor Mary' had thrown herself away gradually came to perceive that the case was very different. As she herself finally put it, Lincoln was her 'Lover, husband, father — all!'

Lincoln had parted from his law partner Stuart in 1841 to begin a three-year association with one Joshua T. Logan. One the ninth of December, 1844, he formed his final Springfield partnership with a young man just admitted to the bar who had once clerked in Speed's store. Red-haired, dandified, emotional but also observant, William H. Herndon was regarded as one of the more idealistic 'wild boys' about Springfield. Utterly loyal to 'Mr. Lincoln' (as he always called him) Billy Herndon did all he could to bridge the growing gap between his prematurely grave partner and Springfield's younger voters.

Lincoln's political ambitions were greater than ever, but his attractions less. Churchmen denounced him as belonging to no church, as having almost fought a duel, and as being soft on drunkenness. (That final charge must have been bitter for the teetotaler to swallow; it arose from an address he'd given at the Temperance Society, urging compassion.) Workingmen complained that Lincoln had married into society and lost the common touch. Abolitionists thought him no friend of theirs, while champions of the southern slave-holding interests already knew him for a hesitant but unbudgeable foe.

Left: *In 1844, Lincoln entered his third law partnership with William H. Herndon, a younger man who had just been admitted to the bar. The partnership, which became more and more successful, lasted until Lincoln's death.*

Right: *William Henry Herndon, though a southerner by birth, like Lincoln, was a Whig politically. He became an ardent abolitionist and prohibitionist, and eventually a radical Republican.*

Although Lincoln earnestly sought the Whig nomination for United States Congressman, he failed to get it until the spring of 1846. Not personal magnetism so much as back room organization gained the prize at last. He'd labored long and hard for previous candidates and, as he kept saying, 'turnabout is fair play.' His Democratic opponent in the ensuing campaign — a circuit-riding Methodist preacher — repeatedly called upon Lincoln to repent his many sins and go to heaven. Instead, Lincoln went to Washington.

The Thirtieth Congress did not convene until

December 6, 1847, after the nation had begun its war with Mexico. Lincoln held his peace on that issue until the 22nd. Then he rose to protest President James K. Polk's assertions that Mexico had begun hostilities by shedding American blood on American soil. Not so, said Lincoln. Polk had ordered American troops into the disputed, Mexican-inhabited Rio Grande territory on purpose to provoke the first bloodshed.

On January 12, 1848, Lincoln again attacked the President. 'I more than suspect,' he said, in one spirited passage, 'that he is deeply conscious of being in the

Right: *James Knox Polk (1795-1849) was nominated for the presidency in 1844. His expansionist platform included plans for the annexation of Texas and reoccupation of the Oregon territory.*

Far right: *Following Polk's instructions, an American army under General Zachary Taylor crossed into Mexican territory and began to build fortifications. When the Mexicans attacked these forts, Polk had his excuse for a war. Winning two battles in two days with few losses made Taylor a popular hero.*

wrong; that he feels the blood of this war, like the blood of Abel, is crying to Heaven against him; that having originally some strong motive — what, I will not stop now to give my opinion concerning — to involve the two countries in a war, and trusting to escape scrutiny by fixing the public gaze upon the exceeding brightness of military glory — that attractive rainbow that arises in showers of blood — that serpent's eye that charms to destroy — he plunged into it, and has swept on and on till, disappointed in his calculation of the ease with which Mexico might be subdued, he now finds himself he knows not where.'

Polk could afford to ignore the freshman congressman. In less than a month his war — which gained the territory of New Mexico and the independent Republic of California for the United States — would end as the whole nation cheered. Lincoln had been marching in the wrong direction, away from the parade — a mistake he would never make again. Home in Springfield the following fall, he found he had already destroyed his own chances of re-election to the House of Representatives.

Below: *The territory of Mexico extended as far as the Pacific Coast. While Taylor and his army were attacking the Mexican army, North American settlers in California were declaring the territory an independent Republic.*

Right: *Antonio Lopez de Santa Anna became commander in chief of the Mexican armies in September 1846. He is best known for commanding the army that attacked the Alamo in San Antonio in 1836.*

VOLUNTEERS!

Men of the Granite State!

Men of Old Rockingham!! the

strawberry-bed of patriotism, renowned for bravery and devotion to Country, rally at this call. Santa Anna, reeking with the generous confidence and magnanimity of your countrymen, is in arms, eager to plunge his traitor-dagger in their bosoms. To arms, then, and rush to the standard of the fearless and gallant **CUSHING**---put to the blush the dastardly meanness and rank toryism of Massachusetts. Let the half civilized Mexicans hear the crack of the unerring New Hampshire rifleman, and illustrate on the plains of San Luis Potosi, the fierce, determined, and undaunted bravery that has always characterized her sons.

Col. **THEODORE F. ROWE**, at No. 31 Daniel-street, is authorized and will enlist men this week for the Massachusetts Regiment of Volunteers. The compensation is **$10 per month---$30 in advance.** Congress will grant a handsome bounty in money and **ONE HUNDRED AND SIXTY ACRES OF LAND.**

Portsmouth, Feb. 2. 1847.

Above: *The call to arms appealed to patriotism, but added the inducement of free land and money, a tradition that goes back to the ancient Romans. Ten dollars a month, at that time, was a decent salary, and the settlement of land also meant the presence of experienced military veterans on the frontier.*

Right: *Following a surprise landing and capture of the powerful fortress of Vera Cruz, an American force under General Winfield Scott headed for Mexico City, defeating Santa Anna's army at several points. Following the battle of Churubusco, Santa Anna asked for an armistice.*

The victorious American army commanded by General Scott entered Mexico City on September 14, 1847. Scott was one of many Mexican War veterans who would later see action in the Civil War, among them Lee, Grant and Stonewall Jackson.

Back in Washington as a lame-duck congressman during the winter of 1849, Lincoln tried to introduce a bill abolishing slavery (with financial compensation to slave-owners) in the District of Columbia. Howled down, he withdrew the proposal. Abolitionist friends at Mrs. Sprigg's boarding house, where Lincoln lodged alone, were not impressed. Lincoln told fewer funny stories at table now. He missed his family; he was again a victim of painful, wracking depression.

Congress adjourned on the fourth of March. Zachary Taylor, for whose Whig candidacy Lincoln had assiduously stumped, was inaugurated as President the following day. Lincoln naturally expected the new administration to pass one or two plum appointments his way; he was ready but not a thing happened.

Upset, he pulled strings to obtain the post of General Land Office Commissioner, which had been promised to Illinois. A Chicago Whig named Justin Butterfield walked off with that prize.

Finally, in September 1849, Taylor's administration offered Lincoln a little something after all. How would he like to serve as Governor of the Oregon Territory at $3000 a year? Lincoln thought about it, until Mary put her foot down. To rule a rain-forest on the far Pacific shore was no part of her ambition — or his either.

Lincoln returned to circuit-riding law practice. At 40, he'd failed to impress himself upon the national political scene. He was anything but resigned, however. Abraham Lincoln would be back, although not for some time.

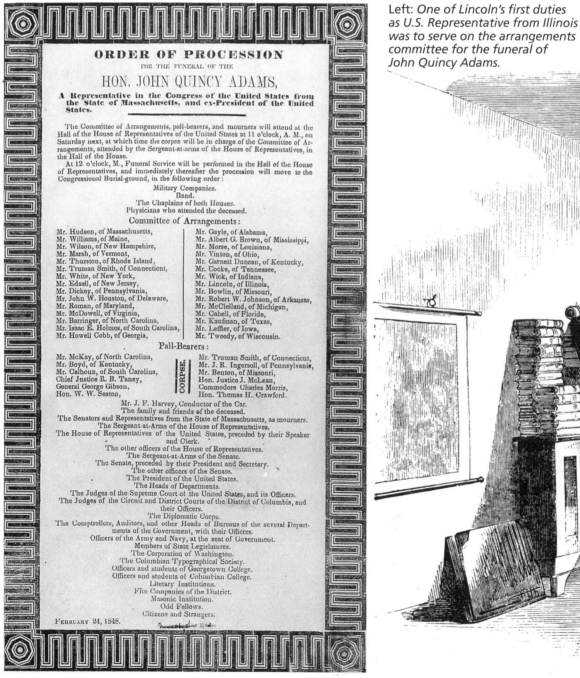

Left: *One of Lincoln's first duties as U.S. Representative from Illinois was to serve on the arrangements committee for the funeral of John Quincy Adams.*

Left: *Lincoln beat two other candidates in the 1846 Congressional race: Peter Cartwright, a Democrat, and Elihu Walker of the Liberty party, which was an abolitionist platform. Lincoln's seat in the House was No. 191, at the back on the right of the center aisle. This would later become the Republican side of the House.*

Below: *Lincoln returned to Springfield, following defeat in his bid for re-election. Renewing his partnership with Billy Herndon was far preferable to a stint in the far west as Governor of the Oregon Territory.*

THE OUTSIDER

Forced to retire from politics at this time, Lincoln devoted himself to his law practice and to improving his mind. As a boy he had puzzled his way through an arithmetic schoolbook on his own. Now he did the same with Euclid's geometry. He studied Shakespeare and the Bible. He subjected his own ideas to the closest analysis, until, as he himself, put the case, he had 'bounded them east, west, north and south.' Meanwhile, Lincoln's activist law partner William Henry Herndon observed, 'melancholy dripped from him as he walked.'

At the beginning of February 1850, the Lincolns' second son Edward died following a two-week illness. Their third child, William Wallace, was born the following December. Then, in January 1851, Thomas Lincoln sickened at the Coles County homestead. Lincoln resisted appeals to visit the dying man, or to attend the funeral. He had nothing in common with his pioneer relations — or nothing that he cared to share any more. However, he did write an acid letter to his stepbrother John Johnston, accusing him of inveterate laziness and insisting that 'Mother's' portion of the farm be rented (rather than sold) in order to assure her a continuing income.

March 1852 saw publication of what was probably the most influential novel ever written. *Uncle Tom's Cabin* — Harriet Beecher Stowe's heartrending tale of slavery — sold 305,000 copies in the United States (and millions worldwide) in its first year alone. Stung Southerners naturally condemned the book as Yankee distortions, but Northern readers swarmed into the 'radical' abolitionist ranks which now violently demanded nothing less than the immediate extirpation of slavery. The South stood firm, as tension grew.

Left: *William Lloyd Garrison (1805-1879), abolitionist publisher of* The Liberator, *was so hated in the South that Georgia offered a $5000 reward for his arrest and conviction.*

Left: *Harriet Beecher Stowe (1811-1896) wrote* Uncle Tom's Cabin *after a three-day visit to Kentucky. This emotional account of slavery from the slave's point of view was published in 1852 and became an instant best-seller, in England as well as in the United States.*

Above: *In a poignant scene from* Uncle Tom's Cabin, *George Shelby frees his slaves. With such characters and actions Mrs. Stowe attempted to be fair-minded, intimating*

that not all Southerners were evil like Simon Legree, the infamous overseer, nor weak like Eva's father St. Clare, who sells his slaves, including Uncle Tom, to recover himself financially.

Right: Uncle Tom's Cabin *was such a success that it suffered adaptation for the stage almost immediately. Still later, it was simplified for younger children. The title page for one edition shows Eliza fleeing across the ice with her child, one of the more dramatic episodes.*

Surprisingly enough, Lincoln's fourth son, born the following April, was named Thomas for his paternal grandfather. One year to the day after 'Tad's' birth, partner Billy Herndon was elected Mayor of Springfield. Then on May 30, 1854 President Franklin Pierce signed the infamous 'Kansas-Nebraska Act' into law. Lincoln saw precisely what this legislation portended. He re-entered politics to fight it, and its sponsor, to the end.

The Act had been sponsored and indeed bullied through Congress by Lincoln's longtime adversary from Illinois state legislature days: Stephen A. Douglas.

The Little Giant, as admirers knew him, was a small, dandified extrovert. Also, he was a dazzling debater and mesmerizing orator with a keen eye for the main chance. Lincoln's opposite in almost every sense, Douglas had gone from strength to strength on the national scene. As a Senator from Illinois and Chairman of the Committee on Territories, Douglas devoted his enormous energies to an important

cause: the opening of the West. The Kansas-Nebraska Act was designed to facilitate that development — at a steep price in liberty and peace.

At that time the population of the South comprised about nine million of whom no less than four million were slaves. Since 1820, slave trade with Africa had been punishable as a capital offense in the United States and most Americans hoped that the institution of slavery would wither away as it had done in other parts of the world. Indeed the Southern plantation aristocracy confronted serious problems. The price of slaves rose after the importation of slaves was forbidden. The main plantation crops of tobacco and cotton seriously depleted the soil; and the world-market price of cotton itself gradually fell. Thus the South found itself economically dependent on the North. Adding insult to injury, her Northern neighbors and creditors kept chorusing their disgust at the South's unconsciously unjust, slave-dependent way of life.

Meanwhile the North's economic network, industrial potential and population were burgeoning. With nearly 14 million inhabitants the North controlled the House of Representatives. But the Senate, with two members from each state, was another matter. The South's 15 states (out of 31 altogether) dominated the

Left: Franklin Pierce (1804-1869), a Northerner by birth, tried to appease the South following his election to the Presidency in 1852 with his support of the Kansas-Nebraska Bill.

Below: The debates between Lincoln and his rival for the Senate, Stephen A. Douglas, over the Kansas-Nebraska Act, were seen as a form of entertainment, frequently caricatured.

Above: *The tobacco plantations enjoyed their heyday in the decades before the Revolution. By the mid-nineteenth century, many of those planters were bankrupt and had sold or freed their slaves. Freeing slaves in one's will was a normal practice in the Tidewater.*

Right: *The cotton plantations of the Deep South were much newer, the soil not so exhausted. Both men and women worked as field hands, and children were brought into the field to do a 'quarter day's work' at the age of twelve.*

Senate by means of 'solid South' voting discipline.

What made the balance precarious was the impending statehood of certain western territories. If they were pro-slavery, these additions would be sure to rescue and vastly augment the fortunes of the slave-holding interests in general. If they were free-states, on the other hand, the carefully maintained Southern domination of the Senate would end and eventual abolition would be assured.

Thus the incipient opening of the West engendered a dangerous, potentially revolutionary uproar of conflicting claims in Washington. Senator Douglas doubtless intended his Kansas-Nebraska Act to reconcile the opposing interests by removing the whole matter from their hands. The Act provided that settlers of the vast area which now comprises Kansas, Nebraska, North Dakota, South Dakota, Montana and northern Colorado should decide for themselves whether to import and keep slaves or not.

'Popular sovereignty' out West was Douglas's rally-ing cry. Or rather — as all abolitionists, 'free-soilers' and humane conservatives (such as Lincoln himself) agreed — it was his inherently vicious acclamation.

When Congress adjourned in the fall of 1854,

Douglas hurried back to Illinois to explain and defend the Kansas-Nebraska Act to his restless, bitterly divided constituents. And now Lincoln retaliated. In Springfield on October 4, he delivered a three-hour address detailing the evils of Douglas's position. Twelve days later, dogging Douglas's own footsteps, he repeated the speech at Peoria, and it was then published in full.

The 'Peoria Address' as this came to be known, was the first great oration of Lincoln's career. Eschewing the dramatic gestures and the profusion of meta-phorical allusions popular at the time, Lincoln plainly and modestly pressed home the following points:

When Southern people tell us they are no more responsible for the origin of slavery than we are, I acknowledge the fact. When it is said that the institution exists, and that it is very difficult to get rid of in any satisfactory way, I can understand and appreciate the saying. I surely will not blame them for not doing what I should not know how to do myself... My first impulse would be to free all the slaves and send them to Liberia, to their own native land. But a moment's reflection would convince me that whatever of high hope (as I think there is) there may be of this in the long run, its sudden execution is impossible....

But all this, to my judgement, furnishes no more excuse for permitting slavery to go into our own free territory than it would for reviving the African slave trade by law. The law which forbids the bringing of slaves from Africa, and that which has so long forbidden the taking of them into Nebraska, can hardly be distinguished on any moral principal, and the repeal of the former could find quite as plausible excuses as that of the latter...

Argue as you will and as long as you will, this is the naked front and aspect of the measure. And in this aspect it could not but produce agitation. Slavery is founded in the selfishness of man's nature — opposition to it in his love of justice. These principles are an eternal antagonism, and when brought into collision so fiercely as slavery extension brings them, shocks and throes and convulsions must ceaselessly follow. Repeal the Missouri Compromise, repeal all compromise, repeal the Declaration of Independence, repeal all past history, you still cannot repeal human nature. It will still be the abundance of man's heart that slavery extension is wrong, and out of the abundance of his heart his mouth will continue to speak.'

Encouraged by the response to this address, Lincoln dared stand for his state legislature's election to the U.S. Senate (for Senators were not yet elected by popular vote). The balloting took place on February 8, 1855, and started well. Lincoln received 45 votes — only six shy of victory — on the first ballot. His closest rival at that point was James Shields, the old pro-Douglas Democrat with whom he'd almost fought a duel in younger days. An anti-Douglas renegade Democrat named Lyman Trumbull meanwhile garnered five votes. But Lincoln's lead eroded as the balloting went on, and in the end he threw his votes to Trumbull — the ultimate victor.

Despite his obvious disappointment Lincoln warmly congratulated Trumbull at a reception the following evening. But Mary Todd Lincoln deliberately snubbed Mr. and Mrs. Trumbull then and forever afterward. The best man had by no means won, in her opinion.

She didn't care for Joshua Speed either. During his four-years as Lincoln's roommate, Speed had been anti-slavery. Since his return to his native Kentucky, he'd changed his mind. Speed now penned a troubled note to his old friend, asserting that he himself would rather see the Union dissolve than cede his slaves at the command of Northern meddlers. The North, Speed protested, had no legitimate interest in the matter. Lincoln, in a letter dated August 24, 1855, replied:

'In 1841 you and I had together a tedious low-water trip on a steamboat from Louisville to St. Louis. You may remember, as I well do, that from Louisville to the mouth of the Ohio there were on board ten or a dozen slaves shackled together with irons. That sight was a continued torment to me, and I see something like it every time I touch the Ohio or any other slave border. It is not fair for you to assume I have no interest in a thing which has, and continually exercises, the power to make me miserable. You ought rather to appreciate how much the great body of the Northern people do crucify their feelings, in order to maintain their loyalty to the Constitution and the Union...

Our progress in degeneracy appears to me to be pretty rapid. As a nation we began by declaring that "all men are created equal." We now practically read it, "all men are created equal, except Negroes. When the Know-Nothings get control, it will read, "all men are created equal, except Negroes and foreigners and Catholics." When it comes to this, I shall prefer emigrating to some country where they make no pretense of loving liberty — to Russia, for instance, where despotism can be taken pure, and without the base alloy of hypocrisy.'

In September 1855, Lincoln was called to Cincinnati as associate council in a patent suit: *McCormack v. Manny*. The chief counsel on Lincoln's side of the case was Edwin M. Stanton, a coarse, self-made man who refused to allow 'the Giraffe' (as he nicknamed Lincoln) any part in the proceedings whatsoever. Lincoln swallowed his pride to stay on as an observer.

Who could have guessed that in the years ahead this same Stanton would serve as President Lincoln's Secretary of War?

Events of the following spring demonstrated the truth of Lincoln's warning that 'shocks and throes and convulsions' were sure to be set in train by the extension of slavery through the Kansas-Nebraska Act. On May 21, 1856, the free town of Lawrence, Kansas, was sacked by a 750-man 'sheriff's posse' of pro-slavers from out-of-state. The violent abolitionist John Brown, who had his own armed gang in Ossawatomie, Kansas, at the time, retaliated by 'executing' five pro-slavery captives. In Washington at almost the same moment, Congressman Preston Brooks of South Carolina assaulted the anti-slavery Senator Charles Sumner of Massachusetts on the Senate floor, beating the seated Sumner over the head with a cane, crippling and nearly killing him.

Left: *Charles Sumner (1811-1874) was a Senator from Massachusetts from 1851 until his death. A staunch abolitionist, he was at one time the only senator opposed to slavery. His uncompromising position enraged another member of Congress, Representative Preston Brooks of South Carolina, who assaulted Sumner in the Senate Chamber.*

Above: *Brooks's attack on Sumner in 1856 left the Senator incapacitated for four years. While the North saw Sumner as a martyr, the South viewed his attacker as one defending his family's good name (Sumner had slighted Brooks's uncle, Andrew Butler, in his speech). The split between North and South was growing ever wider.*

Above: *James Buchanan (1791-1868) served as President Polk's Secretary of State and Ambassador to England before his election in 1856. He denounced slavery as a moral evil, but supported pro-slavery forces, a position that resulted in the Dred Scott case coming before the Supreme Court, Buchanan seemed to believe that the slavery question was strictly a legal one and settled by that tribunal.*

Top right: *On March 6, 1857, the Supreme Court handed down its decision on the case of Dred Scott v Sandford. Scott, a black, was taken from the slave state of Missouri into the free state of Illinois by his master. Scott sued for his freedom, under the laws set out by the Missouri Compromise, and won, but the decision was overturned by the State Supreme Court.*

Bottom right: *Roger Brooke Taney (1777-1864) became Chief Justice of the Supreme Court in 1836. A former slave owner, Taney handed down many decisions that pertained to economics and slavery. His opinion, cited for the majority on Dred Scott, ruled that not only was Scott still a slave, but that no person descended from a slave could be a citizen, and that the Missouri Compromise cited by Scott violated the Constitution.*

Whigs, disaffected Democrats and splinter-groups now flocked together in the North, creating a new party: the Republican. Only by uniting could they hope to break the grip of what Lincoln for one described as the 'Democratic dynasty' in Washington. On May 29, 1856, the Illinois Republicans held a state convention at Bloomington, and Abraham Lincoln was there.

On his way to the convention hall, Lincoln dropped by a jewelry store and fingered through its stock of small-lensed granny glasses, trying one after another on his big nose. Finally locating a pair which seemed to rectify his fine-print-bleared vision somewhat, Lincoln paid 37 and a half cents for it. He was 47.

Lincoln's keynote speech that evening has been described as the most moving of his career so far. No one even thought to take notes, however; it has unfortunately vanished. Some weeks later at the national Republican convention in Philadelphia, John C. Frémont was nominated for President. Lincoln received 110 ballots for the Vice-Presidential post, but lost. He modestly professed to suppose that he had been mistaken for some other, eastern, Lincoln.

Frémont lost the national election to an aging, crafty, pro-South Democrat: James Buchanan. In his inaugural address of March 4, 1857, the new President blandly assured the country that the whole question of slavery extension was soon to be settled by the Supreme Court.

The case in question concerned a slave named Dred Scott, who had sued for his freedom on the ground of having been held for some time in free-state territories where — so Scott contended — he ought to have been treated as a citizen. In fact the Court had already reached its decision on the matter, and Buchanan knew it.

The two Republican Justices voted in Scott's favor, as might be expected. The eight Democrats voted together, with Chief Justice Roger Taney of Maryland coolly explaining that blacks were always 'beings of an inferior order, and altogether unfit to associate with the white race, either in social or political relations; and so far inferior that they had no rights which the white man was bound to respect.' Thus, Taney concluded, the Declaration of Independence had nothing to do with Negroes. Indeed, all subsequent legislation such as the Missouri Compromise and even the Kansas-Nebraska Act which tended to restrict slavery in any shape, form or manner was itself unconstitutional!

In June, Stephen A. Douglas arrived to defend the Dred Scott decision at Springfield, and Lincoln spoke against it. Meanwhile events in Kansas were moving rapidly. Pro-slavers there had created a 'constitutional convention' which framed legislation favoring slavery throughout the territory. However free-state Kansans won control of the state legislature. In effect Kansas had two mutually opposed governments.

To break this deadlock for the South, the administration in Washington jettisoned Douglas's 'popular sovereignty' principle. Matters were arranged so that if

Above: *By 1857, Lincoln was campaigning in earnest for the new Republican Party. After his nomination this was the only picture available to the newspapers. It was taken by Alexander Hesler, who became Lincoln's campaign photographer.*

Right: *By 1858, Springfield had expanded. The former frontier town had shops offering jewelry and silverware. Halfway down the block was a book store, and two buildings beyond was the office of Lincoln and Herndon.*

Kansas voted pro-slavery it could join the Union as a state — otherwise not. This was too much for Douglas to swallow. On the Senate floor he roundly denounced President Buchanan's shenanigans, thus sacrificing his own southern support and irreparably splitting the Democratic party.

Kansas then voted to refuse its pro-slavery constitution even at the price of non-admission to the Union. The count: a hugely lopsided 10,226 to 138. The date: January 4, 1858. The tide had turned. From now on it would flow in slow yet furious turmoil back upon the beleaguered slave-holding interests.

In the spring of 1858, Lincoln experienced the pleasure of returning favors received in the now-distant past. Jack Armstrong, of New Salem's Clary Grove Boys, had given him free hospitality when they were young and Lincoln was desitute. Now Jack was dead, Lincoln learned, and his son Duff was in trouble. So Lincoln wrote to Jack's widow: 'I have just heard of

your deep affliction, and the arrest of your son for murder. I can hardly believe that he can be capable of the crime alleged against him... and gratitude for your long-continued kindness to me in adverse circumstances prompts me to offer my humble services gratuitously on his behalf.'

According to witnesses, young Duff and a youth named James Norris had killed a fellow in a drunken brawl at a place called Virgin's Grove. Norris struck from behind with a wagon-yoke, they said, while Duff dented the victim's brow with a heavy slingshot. When Lincoln entered the case, Norris had already been tried and sent to jail for an eight-year stretch. Defending Duff in court, Lincoln established that the alleged slingshot had been in somebody else's pocket at the time. 'No,' one witness insisted: 'I saw it! The moon shone right down upon Duff's weapon.' Thereupon, Lincoln produced an almanac to prove that the moon had been one hour from setting at the time. Duff was freed.

Preparing for the June 16, 1858, Republican state convention at Springfield, Lincoln wrote a brief address and read it to a group of friends. Some called the speech 'radical,' and even 'dangerous,' but his law partner was ecstatic. 'By God,' Billy Herndon cried, jumping to his feet, 'deliver it just as it reads!' So Lincoln did. It included this crucial paragraph:

We are now far into the fifth year since a policy was initiated with the avowed object and confident promise of putting an end to slavery agitation. Under the operation of that policy, the agitation has not only not ceased but has constantly augmented. In my opinion it will not cease until a crisis shall have been reached and passed. "A house divided against itself cannot stand." I believe this government cannot endure permanently half slave and half free. I do not expect the Union to be dissolved — I do not expect the house to fall — but I do expect it will cease to be divided. It will become all one thing, or all the other. Either the opponents of slavery will arrest the further spread of it, and place it where the public mind shall rest in the belief that it is in the course of ultimate extinction;

Far left: *By the age of 49, Lincoln was a successful lawyer and rising politician. Following the acquittal of Duff Armstrong (one of his most famous cases), Lincoln sat for this ambrotype in the same rumpled holland suit he had worn during the trial.*

Left: *In Congress, dissension between representatives of slave and free states increased. The quarrel was intensified by Supreme Court rulings that contradicted state court convictions, establishing federal precedents in matters that many thought were state affairs.*

or its advocates will push it forward till it shall become alike lawful in all states, old as well as new, North as well as South.

With that, the convention pronounced itself 'Resolved that Abraham Lincoln is the first and only choice of the Republicans of Illinois for the United States Senate, as the successor of Stephen A. Douglas.'

But Douglas had no intention of letting anyone 'succeed' him; he returned home once again to do battle for yet another term as Senator. This time he was welcomed with fireworks, torchlight parades and banners brightly snapping in the breeze. The 'Little Giant' in his white felt hat, the man who dared speak out against Southern chicanery and even to denounce his own party's vindictive President — had never been more popular with the voters than he was now.

How could Lincoln best such a champion?

THE PEOPLE'S CHOICE

On July 9, 1858, Senator Stephen A. Douglas addressed a huge, devoted throng from the balcony of Chicago's Tremont House. Lincoln sat behind him on the balcony, taking notes. Douglas described his political opponent as having dangerously totalitarian ideas. Lincoln's ideological intransigence ignored the rich diversity of interests which was destined to make America great, Douglas averred. Lincoln was on record as saying that the nation must become all slave or all free — a frightening doctrine.

'Uniformity is the parent of despotism the world over,' Douglas explained. Besides, the American government was made 'by the white man, for the white man, to be administered by white men!'

That last lick drew wild cheering from the crowd. But Lincoln remembered and used it alchemically transforming Douglas's white-supremacy dross to purest gold. At Gettysburg, in time to come, President Lincoln was to pledge: 'A new birth of freedom; and that government of the people, by the people, for the people, shall not perish from the earth.'

The evening after Douglas's address, most of the crowd returned to hear Lincoln's rebuttal. Political debates were a prime form of entertainment in those days, and Lincoln was known as a homespun, above-average speaker. With seeming mildness, he summarized Douglas's views. Then came the culminating argument:

> Now I ask you, in all soberness, if all these things, if indulged in, if ratified, if confirmed and endorsed, if taught to our children, and repeated to them, do not tend to rub out the sentiment of liberty in the country, and to transform this government into a government of some other form?
>
> What are these arguments? They are the arguments that kings have made for enslaving the people in all ages of the world. You will find that all the arguments in favor of kingcraft were of this class; they always bestrode the necks of the people — not that they wanted to do it, but because the people were better off for being ridden. That is their argument, and this argument of the judge is the same old serpent that says, 'You work and I eat, you toil and I will enjoy the fruits of it.'

Left: *As Lincoln's fame grew, many photographers requested that he pose for them. Mrs. Lincoln considered this photograph taken in Chicago in 1859 to be 'the best likeness she had ever seen of her husband.'*

The philosophical abyss between Lincoln and Douglas was clear from the start, but no one knew how the voters would react. As rival candidates for the Senate, the two men stumped Illinois county by county and township by township. On top of that they met seven times in formal debate. It was a grueling campaign for both, and by the end Douglas could barely speak above a croak.

Newspapers as far away as New York published many of the debates in full, often with accompanying comments of an exuberantly slanted sort. Republican journals, for example, would report that after a particularly stirring Lincoln oration his friends had carried him in triumph on their shoulders from the podium. The Democratic papers disagreed: Lincoln had been so lambasted by Douglas that he felt unable to stir a limb, so that his handful of severely disappointed followers found themselves compelled to cart the 'tall sucker' bodily from the premises.

Lincoln's actual appearance and style in the debates was acutely observed and described by his partner Billy Herndon:

When he began speaking, his voice was shrill, piping and unpleasant. His manner, his attitude, his dark yellow face, wrinkled and dry, his oddity of pose, his diffident movements — everything seemed to be against him — but only for a short time... He was careless of his dress, and his clothes instead of fitting neatly as did the garments of Douglas on the latter's well-rounded form, hung loosely on his giant frame. As he moved along in his speech he became freer and less uneasy in his movements; to that extent he was graceful. He had a perfect naturalness, a strong individuality, and to that extent he was dignified. He despised glitter, show, set forms, and shams. He spoke with effectiveness and to move the judgement as well as the emotions of men. There was a world of meaning and emphasis in the long bony finger of his right hand as he dotted the ideas on the minds of his hearers.

Election day, November 2, 1858, was cold and rainy. Lincoln had spent four months on the campaign trail; now he slouched tiredly in the Springfield telegraph office with friends to monitor the returns. The Democrats garnered 176,000 popular votes; Republicans 190,000. But that was not a sufficient margin. Thanks to its Democratic holdovers, the state legislature would remain under Democratic control and would return Douglas to the Senate. Lincoln had lost again.

He walked home that night through the ill-lit streets

Left: Stephen Douglas was an old campaigner when he and Lincoln met in a series of debates during the Senate campaign of 1858.

Below: By 1860, in the campaign for the presidency, Lincoln was seen as the victor over Douglas, Breckinridge and John Bell.

Following Lincoln's nomination as the Republican candidate for the Senate in 1858, his Democratic opponent, Stephen Douglas, said: 'Of all the damned Whig rascals about Springfield, Abe Lincoln is the ablest and most honest.... I shall have my hands full. He is the strong man of his party — full of wit, facts and dates — and the best stump speaker, with his droll ways and dry jokes, in the West.'

74

The six debates took place throughout the state of Illinois, and allowed Lincoln to hone and refine his opinion, and especially his stand on slavery. In the late debate — at Alton — Lincoln defined his position and that of his party: 'The real issue in this controversy... is the sentiment on the part of one class that looks upon the institution of slavery as a wrong, and of another class that does not look upon it as a wrong.'

and unpaved walks. 'The path had been worn pigbacked and was slippery,' Lincoln later recalled. 'My foot slipped out from under me... but I recovered and said to myself, "It's a slip and not a fall."'

In fact, although he didn't quite yet know it, Abraham Lincoln was already on the path to the Presidency. The whole nation was aware that Lincoln had stood up to the nation's foremost orator, day after day from summer into autumn, fighting him to a draw.

The South was getting desperate now. In her hunger for slaves she illegally imported some 15,000 of them from Africa during 1859 alone, according to Senator Douglas's figures. Douglas himself expressed deep shock at this revelation.

Below: *John Brown (1800-1859) had been a staunch Abolitionist since 1834. In 1855, he moved to Kansas to work toward bringing that territory into the Union as a free state.*

Right: *The arsenal at Harper's Ferry, was chosen by Brown as his objective for the weapons it contained.*

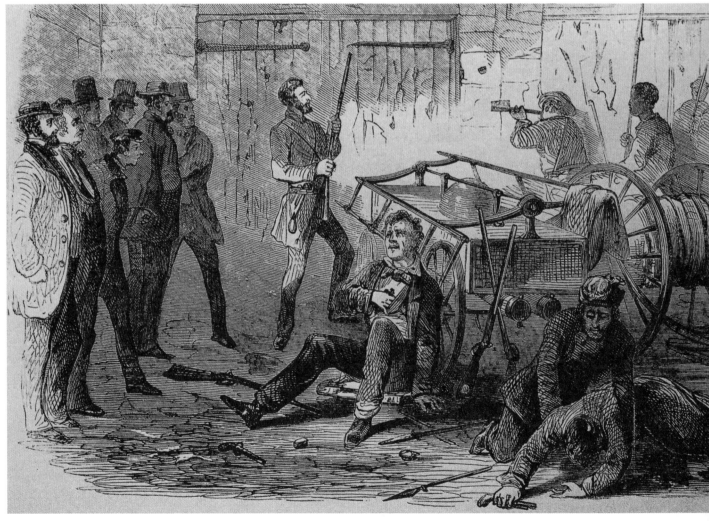

But some abolitionists too were at the end of their tethers, furious with frustration. On October 16, 1859, old John Brown — with only 18 men — captured the Federal arsenal at Harper's Ferry, Virginia. His forlorn hope was to spark a black insurrection throughout the South. Instead, a contingent of United States Marines under the command of Colonel Robert E. Lee captured Brown within two days.

On December 2, 1859, John Brown went to his hanging. The passionate old man sat bound with ropes, atop his own coffin, on a horsedrawn flatbed wagon. (This scene would be unforgettably depicted by the black painter Horace Pippin in 1942.) As he approached the gallows, Brown remarked: 'This is a beautiful country. I never had the pleasure of seeing it before.'

Brown's execution was correct, Lincoln said in a speech the following day: 'Even though he agreed with us in thinking slavery wrong, that cannot excuse violence, bloodshed, and treason.' But Lincoln added an ice-cold warning to the slave-holding South: 'If constitutionally we elect a President, and therefore you undertake to destroy the Union, it will be our duty to deal with you as Old John Brown has been dealt with.'

Far left top: Brown had established a mountain hideout in the Appalachians for escaped slaves and freed blacks. He expected them to lead a series of slave uprisings throughout the South. Following his attack on Harper's Ferry, others flocked to that small town to repulse the expected revolt.

Left: The local militia managed to keep Brown and his last 21 men bottled up in the engine house at the Armory until a troop of U.S. Marines, commanded by Colonel Robert E. Lee, arrived and assaulted 'John Brown's Fort'.

Above: Harper's Ferry was considered a strategic site because of its location at the confluence of the Potomac and Shenandoah Rivers. It was also a major railroad junction.

LINCOLN AS A FLATBOATMAN ON THE MISSISSIPPI RIVER.

QUINCY IN THE DISTANCE.

Peter the Great, to whose genius Russia owes her fame, served an apprenticeship to ship building. Abraham Lincoln has served an apprenticeship to flatboating, and may he yet guide the Ship of State with his own inherent honesty of purpose.

Left: *Brown was tried and convicted of treason. Less than two months after his raid, he was hanged. Although his violent tactics were abhorred by the Abolitionists, they could view him as a martyr to their cause; soon after, Union troops would sing that 'John Brown's Body lies A'moldering in the Grave.'*

Top right: *Life on the Southern plantations, complete with happy, banjo-playing 'darkies' was idealized in a series of popular engravings by Currier and Ives.*

Below right: *Lincoln made two flatboat trips to New Orleans as a young man. The experience was used during his campaign to underline his western origins.*

Following pages: *Campaign posters in 1856 were designed to look like banners. James Buchanan of Pennsylvania and John C. Breckinridge of Kentucky ran on the Democratic ticket. The first Republican presidential candidate was John C. Frémont of California in 1856. His running mate was William L. Dayton of New Jersey.*

JOHN C. FREMONT.
THE REPUBLICANS CHOICE FOR PRESIDENT AND VICE PRESIDENT FROM 1857 TO 1861.

WM L. DAYTON.

GRAND NATIONAL REPUBLICAN BANNER.
FREE LABOR, FREE SPEECH, FREE TERITORY.

ONE COUNTRY _ ONE CONSTITUTION _ ONE DESTINY

UNION

JAMES BUCHANAN.

JOHN C. BRECKENRIDGE.

THE DEMOCRATS CHOICE FOR PRESIDENT AND VICE PRESIDENT FROM 1857 TO 1861.

GRAND NATIONAL DEMOCRATIC BANNER.

PRESS ONWARD,

LITH & PUB. BY N. CURRIER, 152 NASSAU ST. N.Y.

A popular print made after Lincoln's death shows him bearded on his return to Springfield following his nomination. In truth, he began to grow the beard in November of 1860.

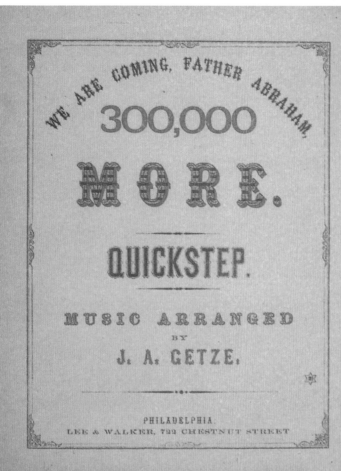

Above: *Once war was declared, the call to arms appeared even on sheet music. This song became one of the most popular Union marching songs.*

Right: *The Union offered such enticements as bounties for joining and land for serving. Money was paid to those who brought in recruits as well. It was said that fortunes could be made enticing immigrants just off the boat. The Union Army was remarkably polyglot when compared to that of the Confederacy.*

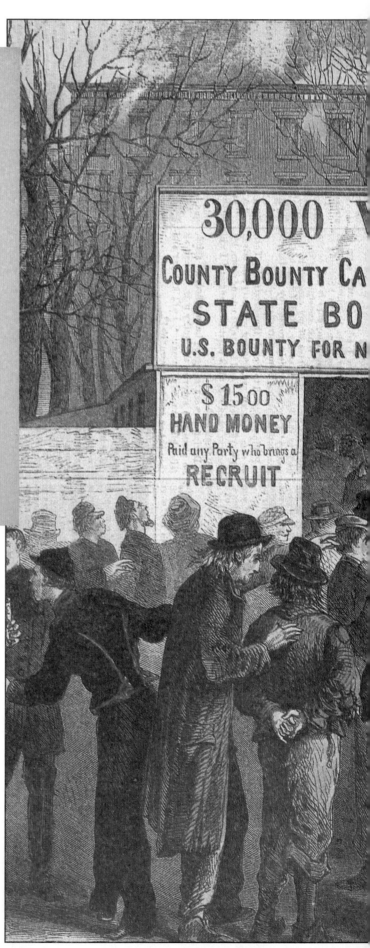

The first militia to respond to Lincoln's call for volunteers was the Massachusetts Sixth. While marching through the city of Baltimore, the Sixth was attacked by a mob. Ironically, it was April 19, the anniversary of the battles of Lexington and Concord. For the next 24 hours, the city was under attack, and Maryland almost seceded.

Left: *The division in the relatively new United States was of great interest in Europe. There were many political cartoons published in newspapers and humor magazines like Punch. In the many independent states of Germany, it was possible to buy a print of the two new presidents together. Such a juxtaposition would have been unthinkable in America.*

Below: *Within the first year of the war, the conflict led to international problems when a U.S. Navy ship, the San Jacinto, stopped the British packet Trent on the high seas and removed two passengers, James Mason and John Slidell, who were traveling to England on behalf of the Confederate Government. When word of this 'outrage' reached the European powers, the Confederacy seemed placed to garner sympathy, perhaps even allied aid.*

The Battle of Gettysburg, considered the turning point of the Civil War, lasted three days. Lee's gamble of extending his army into Pennsylvania, perhaps to surround and attack Washington from the north, was lost. Casualties on both sides were very high, over a third of the Confederate force dead or wounded, and nearly as many Union soldiers.

Left and below: *In the middle of the war came the presidential campaign of 1864. The Republicans were by no means united behind Lincoln; a week before the convention, a splinter group calling themselves 'the Radical Democracy' nominated General John C. Frémont for President, and General John Cochrane for Vice-President. Frémont withdrew after repeated urgings from other members of the Republican party about six weeks before the election. The Democratic candidate was another General, George B. McClellan, who had been in retirement since November 1862, when Lincoln had relieved him of command following his abortive attack on Richmond and Petersburg.*

Opposite: *After four years of war, the popular prints featuring reunification were published. Lincoln rides in triumph over the states now 'one and indivisible,' while Jefferson Davis dismounts.*

GEN⸱ JOHN C. FREMONT.
FOR PRESIDENT.

GEN⸱ JOHN COCHRANE.
FOR VICE PRESIDENT.

GEN⸱ GEO. B. McCLELLAN.
FOR PRESIDENT.

HON⸱ GEO. H. PENDLETON.
FOR VICE PRESIDENT.

Above: 'Furling the Flag' became one of the icons of the shattered South. Despite the bravery of her forces, the Confederacy was a lost cause before the first shot was fired at Fort Sumter.

Left: *Though painted years later, The Peacemakers conveyed those days in early April 1865 when Lincoln visited Richmond, Virginia, to plan the peace with Generals Sherman (left) and Grant, and Admiral David Porter (right).*

Right: *The so-called Cooper Union portrait by Mathew Brady, taken only hours before Lincoln's address to the Young Men's Central Republican Union in New York. Lincoln himself said 'Brady and the Cooper Union Institute made me President.' Following this impressive speech, Lincoln traveled through New England.*

On a crucial visit to New York City the following winter, Lincoln struck the same note of moderation coupled with terrible firmness. Earlier in the day — it was February 27, 1860 — he had dropped by Mathew Brady's studio to pose for a publicity shot which could be used to make him better known in the East. Brady's first portrait shows Lincoln standing tall, solemn, and seemingly ready to take oath upon a stack of books.

'Wrong as we think slavery is,' Lincoln told the 1500 people who crowded into Cooper Union that snowy evening, 'we can yet afford to let it alone where it is, because that much is due to the necessity arising from its actual presence in the nation; but can we, while our votes will prevent it, allow it to spread into the national Territories, and to overrun us here in these free states? If our sense of duty forbids this, then let us stand by our duty.... Neither let us be slandered from our duty by false accusations against us, nor frightened from it by menaces of destruction to our government, nor of dungeons to ourselves. Let us have faith that right makes might, and in that faith let us to the end dare to do our duty as we understand!'

That ringing conclusion, so like a battle hymn in its dark yet righteous tone, triggered a tumultuous standing ovation for Lincoln. From then on the sharp insiders of Republican party politics regarded Lincoln as an awkward but upright, crowd-pleasing, potentially useful compromise candidate on the national level. They sensed that they might soon have need for such a man, since the better-known Eastern politicians were so often at odds with each other.

Lincoln's impression in the eyes of influential journalists such as Horace Greeley, and backroom political kingmakers such as Thurlow Weed, was enormously advanced by events at the Illinois Republican State Convention at Decatur on May 9, 1860. Lincoln's cousin and Mississippi flatboating comrade, John Hanks turned up at the convention hall carrying a couple of fence-rails which he claimed Lincoln had split on the Sangamon bottom 30 years earlier. Instantly, thanks to Hanks's corny stunt, Lincoln's political image was transformed. The careworn, glum-looking lawyer in the stovepipe hat became a 'natural,' a hardswinging rustic giant of the prairie, prepared to fight for what was obviously right; in short, 'The Railsplitter Candidate. '

Nine days later, the Republican National Convention meeting in Chicago rejected half a dozen more 'distinguished' candidates to nominate the fast-rising railsplitter for President. Lincoln himself had passed

the day 'quietly,' back in Springfield. His heart at least must have been unquiet. He played a little handball with some friends, one of whom later described Lincoln's moment of triumph:

A messenger from the telegraph office entered with the decisive dispatch in his hand.... Mr. Lincoln read it in silence, then aloud. After exchanging greetings and receiving congratulations from those around him, he strove to get out of the crowd, and as he moved off, he remarked to those near him: 'Well, there is a little woman who will be interested in this news, and I will go home and tell her.'

Lincoln stayed in Springfield throughout the summer, avoiding campaigning so as not to commit

In the decades before the Civil War, a number of slaves did escape. With the aid of an ardent group of abolitionists known as the Underground Railroad, thousands of slaves went north to start new lives in Canada or the free states. Abolitionists would meet a shipment of slaves, feed and clothe them, then pass them on to the next safe house. Frequently bounty hunters would be sent after the escapees, hoping to catch them before they left a slave state.

himself to a particular position. The long-dominant Democrats had meanwhile doomed their own chances of success against him by fielding two Presidential candidates at once. Douglas was the choice of the Democrats' northern wing only. The South would throw away its still considerable voting power on John C. Breckinridge of Kentucky. So Lincoln knew that he was a shoo-in for President. Yet the prospect must have been awesome. Angry southerners freely warned that Lincoln's election would destroy the whole sense of the Union for them.

Meanwhile the portraitist George Peter Alexander Healy, commissioned by Congress to paint Presidents at $1000 per head, with great foresight appeared in Springfield and asked Lincoln to pose for him. An observer recorded that Lincoln *sat to the artist with his*

right foot on top of the left and both feet turned inward — pigeon fashion — round-shouldered, looking grim as fate, sanguinity in his expression, occasionally breaking into a broad grin.... He chatted, told stories, laughed at his own wit — and the humor of others — and in one way or another made a couple of hours pass merrily.'

Healy himself recalled that Lincoln perused his voluminous correspondence as he sat, and once burst out laughing at a letter from a small girl. 'As a painter, Mr. Healy,' Lincoln suggested, 'you should be the judge between this unknown correspondent and me. She complains of my ugliness. It is allowed to be ugly in the world, but not as ugly as I am. She wishes me to put on false whiskers to hide my horrible lantern jaws. Will you paint me with false whiskers? No?'

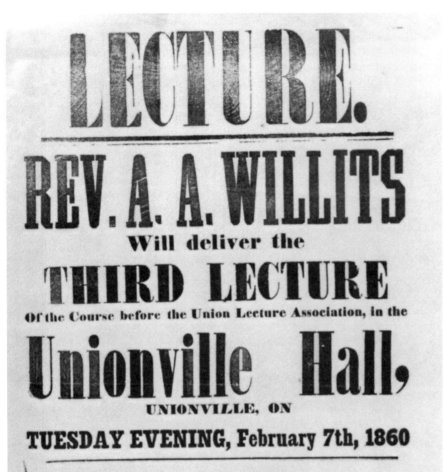

Left: *Three weeks before the Cooper Union speech, the Rev. A. A. Willits spoke on* The Age and the Man for It. *The man in question was Lincoln.*

Below: *In the weeks following the convention in Chicago, the Republican machine moved to make its new candidate a familiar face to the American populace.*

Above: *Lincoln's running mate was Senator Hannibal Hamlin of Maine, a Democrat who had left that party in disgust following repeal of the Missouri Compromise.*

Right: *To satisfy the demand for Lincoln's picture, music publishers frequently placed it on the covers of political song sheets.*

Following spread: *The Republicans met in a specially constructed building known as the Wigwam for the Convention in May 1860.*

He was 51. Healy's bare-cheeked likeness seems to show a younger man whose colorless small eyes, prominent nose, and large right ear are all made up for by the tense, determined mouth and chin. But Lincoln would seem to have accepted the little girl's judgment on his 'ugliness.' Although he did not go so far as to hide behind false whiskers, he grew real ones without delay. So Healy's portrait was to be the last total exposure of the Lincoln physiognomy. Lincoln's personal tenacity and willpower are plain to see in this painting. The deeper layer which comprised his austere yet compassionate and rather patriarchal spirit is more apparent in some of the later photographs.

The nation voted on November the sixth: 1,866,000 for Lincoln, 1,377,000 for Douglas, and 850,000 for Breckinridge. The South, roundly defeated in the battle of the ballot-box, now began re-grouping for a different war. Lincoln's inauguration was still four months off, and some thought that it might never take place. Bumbling old Buchanan himself was heard to moan: 'I am the last President of the United States!'

'Well,' said Horace Greeley in his mighty-voiced New York Tribune, 'if the South wishes to secede, why not?' It would save the nation embarrassment, he thought, and many abolitionists agreed. They could no longer bear the necessity of compromise, in Washington or anywhere else, with slave-holders.

Meanwhile the few remaining pro-Union Southerners — notably Senator John J. Crittenden of Kentucky — strove for some kind of accommodation that would satisfy most white people. For example, said Crittenden, why not extend the old Missouri Compromise line straight across the nation? Thus slavery would be allowed comfortable expansion south of 36°

Below: Among the political demonstrations during the convention and before the election were those by the Wide-Awakes — young Republicans who marched in zig-zag formations bearing lanterns, to imitate the pattern of a split-rail fence.

Right: The symbols of Lincoln's pioneer background — the ax, a wedge, a maul, and the primitive steering and rigging devices of the flat boats — were found everywhere on campaign literature and popular music.

DEDICATED TO THE

HON. ABRAHAM LINCOLN.

CHESTER COUNTY TIMES
EXTRA

WEST CHESTER, PA., NOVEMBER 7, 1860.

A Clean Sweep !

CORRUPTION ENDED !!

THE COUNTRY REDEEMED !

Secession is Rebuked !!!

LET THE TRAITORS RAVE !

LINCOLN'S ELECTED.
AND
WHO'S AFRAID?

PENNSYLVANIA,	60,000 majority.
NEW YORK,	40,000 "
OHIO,	40,000 "
INDIANA,	8,000 "
RHODE ISLAND,	5,000 "
CHESTER COUNTY,	3,000 "

VIRGINIA has gone for BELL.
NORTH CAROLINA has gone for BRECK'GE.

We hail with the breaking day the joyful news that ABRAHAM LINCOLN is elected President of the United States, and send it greeting to our fellow citizens! The reign of the Slave Oligarchy has ended, and corruption must cease. Let us rejoice as we read.

BY TELEGRAPH.

[Special Dispatches for Chester Co. Times.]

The returns from the interior of the State were procured by Mr. U. H. Painter, Superintendent of the Telegraph line.

PENNSYLVANIA.—Schuylkill county gives 1500 for Lincoln—a gain of 865 over Curtin. Snyder 650 for Lincoln.

Union gives 1100 for Lincoln.

Franklin county gives 1100 for Lincoln.

In Tyrone City—Blair county—Lincoln's majority is 25, a gain of 3 for the Fusionists.

Huntingdon Boro'—Lincoln gains 65 over Curtin.

Lancaster City gives 88 majority for Lincoln. There were 276 straight Douglas votes.

Danville—Lincoln gains 78.

Dauphin county—1600 majority for Lincoln. Harrisburg gains 200 over Curtin's vote.

Mount Joy Borough, gives Lincoln 490 majority—a heavy gain.

Lancaster county 8000 for Lincoln.

Alleghaney county—10,000 for Lincoln.

Berks county 1000 for Fusion—a great gain for the Republicans.

Westmoreland—100 to 150 for Lincoln.

Union county—437 maj for Lincoln.

Centre county—500 majority for Lincoln.

Brooklyn city, N. Y., gives 10,000 for Fusion.

Philad'a, Nov. 6, 10.00 P. M.—It is rumored here that Speaker Pennington is defeated.

12.45 A. M.—The following dispatch has just been received from Gov. SEWARD, from Auburn :—"I assert from reliable authority, that Lincoln has carried the State of New York by 60,000 majority. Lincoln's election is conceded on all hands."

Philad'a, Nov. 7, 1 30 P. M.—New York City gives 28,1 4 against Lincoln.

Messrs Wood, King, Taylor and Ward, all locofocos, are elected to Congress from New York city. Eli Thayer is reported to be defeated in Massachusetts by the regular Republican nominee.

LINCOLN'S ELECTION IS NOW CONCEDED BY ALL PARTIES.

2 00 A M.—Philadelphia City gives 15,000 majority for "Old Abe."

CHESTER COUNTY.—We have only 30 townships reported. They give Lincoln 2400 majority. The townships yet to hear from will swell this majority to 3000. The following is the Vote as far as heard from :

VOTE IN CHESTER CO. FOR PRESIDENT.

TOWNSHIPS.	L & H.	FUSION	DOUG.	BELL.
Pocopson,	60	22	00	00
West Goshen,	101	40	2	3
East Goshen,	120	36	2	1
W. Chester—N. Ward	284	128	25	12
" S.	230	91	19	15
Kennett Boro',	96	25	00	00
Kennett,	162	64	1	0
West Bradford,	195	71	2	0
E. Whiteland,	98	87	1	2
E. Caln,	122	40	3	0
Downingtown Bo.	93	72	0	0
Darlington's,	88	47	5	0
Birmingham,	47	31	0	0
W. Whiteland,	147	81	0	6
Phœnixville,	377	279	31	58
Schuylkill,	167	62	3	1
E. Marlborough,	218	61	2	4
Londongrove,	221	38	0	0
E. Bradford,	148	26	12	0
Wallace,	98	39	0	0
Upper Uwchlan,	81	82	0	10
Uwchlan,	104	55	2	3
E. Fallowfield,	175	97	0	0
Newlin,	109	24	0	0
W. Brandywine,	120	65	4	0
W. Pikeland,	57	131	2	0
Honeybrook,	218	137	7	0
E. Brandywine,	86	87	0	5
New London,	84	67	0	3

WIDE AWAKE

LINCOLN ELECTED !

FELLOW-CITIZENS OF BELL COUNTY. The crisis is upon us. Our Abolition enemies who are pledged to prostrate the white freemen of the South down to equality with negroes—to give negroes the right to vote, hold office, serve on juries and sit at our tables as the equals of our sons and daughters, have elected Abe Lincoln to carry out their hellish schemes for our ruin. Is there a white man in Texas so base, so degraded, as to submit to such a ruler and such an enemy? Let one universal shout of NO ! ascend from every voice in the State. Let us not be behind our brethren in other States and other parts of Texas in rallying to the standard of Liberty and Equality for white men. Let us meet and confer together as a band of brothers.— We invite all our fellow-citizens of Bell County to meet at the Court House in Belton, on Saturday, the 17th day of Nov., 1860. Already a large number of our citizens have enrolled themselves into a company to aid in protecting our sacred and endangered rights to "life, liberty and the pursuit of happiness." McLennan, our sister county, has already raised three companies. Let no stain attach to Bell county—let her sons at once take a high stand—and the day is not distant when we shall be proud of such action. Come one ! Come all !! Let the spirit of '76 and '36 animate every heart.

MEMBERS OF BELL CO. COMPANY.

P. S.—Wm. H. Parsons and Judge Davis, of Waco, (the latter a warm supporter of Bell and Everett,) will address the meeting.

THE LADIES OF BELL COUNTY ARE SPECIALLY INVITED TO ATTEND.

30′ latitude, and blessed peace would prevail.

Lincoln said nothing in public; privately he was adamant. In a carefully worded note dated December 17, Lincoln outlined his own position for the shrewd Eastern string-puller Thurlow Weed:

'Should the convocation of governors of which you speak seem desirous to know my views on the present aspect of things, tell them you judge from my speeches that I will be inflexible on the territorial question; that I probably think either the Missouri line extended, or Douglas's and Eli Thayer's popular sovereignty, would lose us everything we gain by the election...

I believe you can pretend to find but little, if anything, in my speeches about secession. But my opinion is, that no State can in any way lawfully get out of the Union without the consent of the others; and that it is the duty of the President and other government functionaries to run the machine as it is.'

Three days after this note was written, South Carolina seceded from the Union. Mississippi, Florida, Alabama, Georgia, Louisiana and finally Texas followed. Then, on February 4, 1861, at Montgomery, Alabama, delegates from all of the seceding states except Texas met to form their own Confederate Government.

Left: *The election of 1860 split the country. The Northern papers, witness the* Chester (Pennsylvania) County Times, *acclaimed the results, even giving the majority results from county to county. The South fell more into line with the broadside (near left) from Bell County, Texas, and began to raise companies 'to aid in protecting our sacred and endangered rights to "life, liberty and the pursuit of happiness."' Most of the South was ignorant of Lincoln, and swayed by the anti-Lincoln propaganda that portrayed him as an ardent abolitionist threatening Southern institutions.*

Right: *In 1860, the year of the election, Lincoln was 51. A photograph taken at the time of the convention reveals a man in the prime of life. Lincoln's partner, William Herndon, said of this portrait: 'There is the peculiar curve of the lower lip, the lone mole on the right cheek, and a pose of the head so essentially Lincolnian; no other artist ever caught it.'*

CHARLESTON

MERCURY

EXTRA:

Passed unanimously at 1.15 o'clock, P. M. December 20th, 1860.

AN ORDINANCE

To dissolve the Union between the State of South Carolina and other States united with her under the compact entitled "The Constitution of the United States of America."

We, the People of the State of South Carolina, in Convention assembled, do declare and ordain, and it is hereby declared and ordained,

That the Ordinance adopted by us in Convention, on the twenty-third day of May, in the year of our Lord one thousand seven hundred and eighty-eight, whereby the Constitution of the United States of America was ratified, and also, all Acts and parts of Acts of the General Assembly of this State, ratifying amendments of the said Constitution, are hereby repealed; and that the union now subsisting between South Carolina and other States, under the name of "The United States of America," is hereby dissolved.

THE

UNION

IS

DISSOLVED!

A week later, Lincoln departed from Springfield. He was on his way to administer, and to succour if he possibly could, a nation which had just cut itself in two. Meanwhile, on that dark morning of February 11, at Springfield's railroad depot, a cold drizzle fell. Lincoln stood looking gaunt and bleak upon the observation platform of the special train which would take him to Washington. Addressing the black umbrellas and the tearstained upturned faces below he said:

No one, not in my situation, can appreciate my feeling of sadness at this parting. To this place, and the kindness of these people, I owe everything. Here I have lived a quarter of a century, and have passed from a young man to an old man. Here my children have been born, and one is buried. I now leave, not knowing when or whether ever I may return, with a task before me greater than that which rested upon Washington. Without the assistance of that Divine Being who ever attended him, I cannot succeed. With that assistance, I cannot fail. Trusting in Him who can go with me, and

remain with you, and be everywhere for good, let us confidently hope that all will yet be well. To his care commending you, as I hope in your prayers you will command me, I bid you an affectionate farewell.

Mrs. Lincoln was not aboard. Rumor related that Lincoln's 'little lady' had thrown a tantrum and refused to come. However, she and the children joined the train at Indianapolis. It progressed with ceremonial slowness, stopping for Lincoln to address enthusiastic crowds which gathered at Cincinnati, Columbus, Cleveland, Pittsburgh, Buffalo, Albany, and New York. But Lincoln kept his speeches brief and vague, expressing hopes which he cannot have felt. His own looks belied what he said. A reporter observed:

'As the carriage in which he sat passed slowly by on Fifth Avenue, he was looking weary, sad, feeble and faint. My disappointment was excessive; so great, indeed, as to be almost overwhelming. He did not look to me to be the man for the hour.'

STORMING THE CASTLE
"OLD ABE" ON GUARD.

Published by Currier & Ives, 152 Nassau St. N.Y.

Left: *A month after the election, South Carolina, seceded from the Union. Congress, in the waning weeks of the Buchanan Adminis-tration, attempted to reconcile differences by restoring the Missouri Compromise.*

Above: *Lincoln, the 'Wide-Awake' watchman, confronts Douglas unlocking the door with keys of non-intervention and the Nebraska Bill; Bell waits to slide in behind him. Buchanan, in the window, tries to pull Breckinridge in before the latter pulls him out.*

Left: *After the election, Southern sympathizers still viewed Lincoln with ridicule. A fictitious account in the* New York Times, *describing Lincoln as sneaking into Washington for the inauguration disguised in a long coat and scotch cap, caught the imagination of cartoonist Adalbert Volck of Baltimore. In truth, Lincoln had traveled to Washington a day ahead of schedule, at the urging of Allan Pinkerton, to avoid possible threats of assassination.*

At that point, Lincoln had just been informed of Jefferson Davis's inauguration as President of the Confederate States of America. Further discouraging news awaited him at his next stop, Philadelphia. There the legendary detective Allan Pinkerton apprised Lincoln of a plot to board the President-elect's sleeping-car as it slowly passed through Baltimore, and murder him in his berth. To forestall any such attempt, Lincoln secretly altered his schedule, reaching Washington a day earlier than planned.

Left: *The president of the new Confederate States of America, Jefferson Davis (1808-1889) of Mississippi, a former Senator, was inaugurated on February 18, 1861 in Montgomery, Alabama, the temporary capital.*

Below: *The Confederacy managed to put together a government and a cabinet before Lincoln left Springfield. The South not only had able legislators like Davis and Judah Benjamin, later to be Secretary of the Treasury, but the cream of the officer corp — men like Robert E. Lee, Pierre G. T. Beauregard and Raphael Semmes.*

Shortly before noon on March 4, 1861, President Buchanan's open ceremonial carriage stopped in front of Willard's Hotel. The old prevaricator stepped inside to meet his successor. Emerging together, they rode down Pennsylvania Avenue under close cavalry guard. Riflemen stationed on the housetops, and soldiers drawn up around the square in front of the unfinished Capitol building, stood anxious watch. A long boarded passageway had been constructed to protect the Presidential party from assault on its way to the speaker's platform.

Above: *Washington in 1861 was still under construction, since the city wasn't begun until 1791. The Capitol building was started in 1793. By the time of Lincoln's first inauguration, the Capitol still lacked a dome, and in places the ravages of the War of 1812 were still visible.*

Right: *Lincoln's inauguration was a much less formal occasion than today's ceremony. Tickets on the balcony were available to all comers, and most people thought nothing of standing through the ceremony and subsequent orations.*

Following spread: *The oath of office was administered by Chief Justice Roger Taney, whose decision in the Dred Scott Case had intensified the division between North and South.*

Left: *Two days after arriving in Washington, as President-elect, Lincoln visited both houses of Congress, an unprecedented occurrence.*

Lincoln did not know what to do with his top hat. His ancient foe Stephen A. Douglas smilingly took it from him. Shrivelled and shaking, Chief Justice Taney croakingly administered the Oath of Office. Field-batteries thunderously saluted, as the new President rose to speak:

One section of our country believes slavery is right, and ought to be extended, while the other believes it is wrong, and ought not to be extended. This is the only substantial dispute.... Physically speaking, we cannot separate. We cannot remove our respective sections from each other, nor build an impassable wall between them. A husband and wife may be divorced and go out of the presence and beyond the reach of each other; but the different parts of our country cannot do this....

In your hands, my dissatisfied fellow-countrymen, and not in mine, is the momentous issue of civil war. The government will not assail you. You can have no conflict without being yourselves the aggressors. You have no oath registered in heaven to destroy the government, while I shall have the most solemn one to 'preserve, protect, and defend it.'

Although practically certain that war must come, Lincoln was determined not to fire the first shot.

THE COMPASSIONATE WARRIOR

Lincoln selected a member of the eastern establishment, William H. Seward to serve as his Secretary of State. Stubborn Salmon P. Chase was his choice for Secretary of the Treasury. When friends protested that Chase regarded himself as 'a bigger man' than the President, Lincoln responded:

'Well, if you know of any other men who think they are bigger than I am, let me know. I want to put them all in my Cabinet.'

His Postmaster General, Montgomery Blair, had been the attorney for Dred Scott before the Supreme Court. Edward Bates of Missouri, the new Attorney General, was regarded as a statesman of the law. However Lincoln's Secretaries of War, of the Interior, and of the Navy (Simon Cameron, Caleb B. Smith and Gideon Welles, respectively) had been appointed to fulfill political commitments. Despite this, Lincoln seemed deferential to his whole Cabinet. The gaunt good man out of the West appeared badly depressed, his worldly new associates agreed, and uncertain how to proceed.

The situation at Fort Sumter constituted the immediate sticking-point. Still in Union hands, this island fort commanded the harbor entrance to Charleston, South Carolina. Confederate shore-batteries in turn threatened the fort. No shots had yet been fired, but the Union garrison was running low on food. Sumter would soon be starved out unless resupplied.

On March 15, 1861, 11 days after his Inauguration, Lincoln asked his Cabinet whether to attempt a rescue-mission or not. Only Blair and Chase felt it might succeed. So Lincoln waited.

Left: *In a photograph taken at an early sitting at Mathew Brady's Gallery in Washington, Lincoln's right hand is uncomfortably swollen from shaking hands with thousands of well-wishers since his arrival the previous morning.*

GIDEON WELLES, Sec of the Navy.   MONTGOMERY BLAIR, P.M.Gen!   CALEB B SMITH, Sec of the Interior
SALMON P CHASE, Sec of the Treasury.   WILLIAM H. SEWARD, Sec of State.   EDWARD BATES, Att'y Gen!   EDWIN M. STANTON, Sec of War.
PRESIDENT LINCOLN.

PRESIDENT LINCOLN AND HIS CABINET.
IN COUNCIL, SEPT. 22ND 1862, ADOPTING THE EMANCIPATION PROCLAMATION, ISSUED JAN'Y. 1ST 1863.

Above: *Most of Lincoln's cabinet remained the same during two administrations, although Stanton replaced Simon Cameron after the latter resigned following complaints regarding the awarding of army contracts.*

Top right: *William H. Seward (1801-1872) was Secretary of State for Lincoln and his successor. He was also responsible for the purchase of Alaska from Russia in 1867.*

Bottom right: *Salmon P. Chase (1808-1873) served Lincoln as Secretary of the Treasury during his first administration. Chase had presidential ambitions, but failed to garner the Republican nomination in 1864. He was then appointed Chief Justice by the man he had tried to supplant.*

Then, on April 1, Secretary Seward presented Lincoln with an astonishing memo entitled 'Some Thoughts for the President's Consideration.' Its wording was roundabout, but Seward's leading propositions were as follows:

'First, hold other forts but let Sumter go. Second, bury the slavery issue while waving the flag for Union. Third, provoke some foreign war in order to re-unite the nation against a common enemy!' To do all this, Seward brashly and ungrammatically concluded, 'is not my special province, but I neither seek to evade nor assume responsibility.'

With Lincoln's administration less than one month old, Seward had already begun secret and totally unauthorized negotiations with Confederate agents. He seemed to think that civil war could be averted, but not by the President. He — Seward — was the man to do it. A lesser President might well have sacked his would-be-slick Secretary of State for impertinence, but

Lincoln seems to have reasoned that Seward — like himself — was simply learning on the job. Lincoln penned this gently magisterial response:

'When a general line of policy is adopted, I apprehend there is no danger of its being changed without good reason, or continuing to be a subject of unnecessary debate; still, upon points arising in its progress I wish, and suppose I am entitled to have, the advice of all the Cabinet.'

Five days later, Lincoln ordered a relief expedition to sail to Fort Sumter. At the same time he sent a special messenger to Charleston with these words for South Carolina's Confederate Governor, Francis W. Pickens:

'I am directed by the President of the United States to notify you to expect an attempt will be made to supply Fort Sumter with provisions only; and that, if such an attempt be not resisted, no effort to throw in men, arms, or ammunition, will be made without further notice, or in case of an attack upon the fort.'

Clearly, Lincoln had composed this message with extreme care. From the viewpoint of the Union and the North, it seemed a crisp yet chivalrous announcement of pacific intent; whereas to the Southern Confederacy it carried a barely veiled burden of threat. The message could be read as a signal for outright war 'on further notice.' Governor Pickens elected to strike first.

On April 12, 1861, Confederate shore batteries began a bombardment of Fort Sumter. The outcome was inevitable but the garrison made a gallant stand before surrendering.

Now, in the North and in the South alike, martial spirits soared. Two days after the surrender of Fort Sumter, Stephen A. Douglas bustled into the President's office to pledge unstinting support and to suggest that Lincoln mobilize 200,000 militia instead of 75,000 as planned. Douglas was on the point of departure for Illinois in order to rally Union forces there. The old adversaries shook hands. Within two months, the 'Little Giant' would be dead of 'acute rheumatism' (at 48) in Chicago's summer heat.

As Lincoln had once accused President Polk of provoking the war with Mexico, so he himself confronted similar charges of having maneuvered the country into war. But Lincoln was painfully aware — and almost all historians agree — that no merely human agency could have forestalled the coming struggle. Thus his first business as a statesman and strategist had been to goad his opponents into making the initial hostile move. 'Then and thereby,' as he informed Congress 'the assailants of the Government began the conflict of arms.'

Virginia, Tennessee, Arkansas and North Carolina now found themselves forced to take one side or the other. As expected, all four elected to join the Confederacy. However, the mountainous borderlands comprising western Virginia and eastern Tennessee inhabited by impoverished Scotch Irish settlers opted

Left: *Fort Sumter, in the harbor of Charleston, South Carolina, was the last remaining Federal garrison in the Confederacy. Commanded by Major Robert Anderson, Fort Sumter had been in a state of siege since December 1860. Following a Confederate demand for surrender, the commander agreed, provided the fort was not relieved. Knowing that a Federal gunboat was on its way, the Confederate force notified Major Anderson that an attack would begin shortly. Sumter was bombarded for over a day before surrendering. The Civil War had begun.*

Above and right: *The first engagement was news. Many magazines and papers sent special correspondents to South Carolina to cover the attack. The wash drawings of William Waud (right) are exceptionally lively. Here Waud sketches the mounting of Confederate artillery.*

FOURTH REGIMENT
NEW HAMPSHIRE

VOLUNTEERS.

ABLE BODIED MEN WANTED
FOR THE FOURTH REGIMENT.

The subscribers having been appointed Recruiting Officers, will open a Recruiting Office at

Where they will enlist all who would like to rally around the OLD STARS AND STRIPES, the emblem of America's Freedom.

$10 BOUNTY WILL BE ALLOWED!

Regular Army pay and Rations to commence on taking the oath.

Lieut. J. M. CLOUGH,
Sergt. W. B. ROWE.

Sept. 1861.

Fogg, Hadley & Co., Printers, Concord.

Left: *Following Fort Sumter, the Union needed an army quickly, and volunteers were summoned from all over the North.*

Above: *While evacuating the Federal Navy Yard in Norfolk, Virginia, Union troops burned it. Many of the buildings were still in ruins at the end of the war.*

to remain within the Union. West Virginia would be proclaimed a separate state on June 20, 1863. Meanwhile, patriotism ran high. The President's call for 75,000 volunteers, published on April 15, 1861, brought far more than the required number of Northerners flocking to defend their flag.

Almost immediately, Lincoln agreed to a blockade of Confederate ports, to maintain the Union's 'territorial integrity against its own domestic foes.' Consistently successful, despite blockade runners, this strategy forced the Confederacy to import manufactured goods at increasingly higher prices, and made the export of Southern cash crops, such as cotton and tobacco more and more difficult, with disastrous results on the economy of the struggling nation.

Throughout the summer of 1861 the city of Washington stood in danger. Across the Potomac in Virginia, the Confederate banners on Arlington Heights were visible from the windows of the White House. The Federal arsenal over at Harpers' Ferry, and the ships in the U.S. Navy yard near Norfolk, had been hastily burned to keep them from rebel hands. Riots in Baltimore prevented some Northern reinforcements from getting through. If Maryland espoused the southern cause, the Capital would be surrounded and fall.

But Maryland stood firm; the railroad to the north reopened. More and more Northern troops pulled in at Washington's Union Station, trailed by miles of freight and artillery mounted on flatcars. Soldiers bedded down in the Capitol Building, and even on the White House lawn. The city was transformed into an armed camp, as confidence returned.

Right: *The first international crisis of the Lincoln Administration took place when the U.S.S.* San Jacinto *stopped the British packet* Trent, *en route from the West Indies to England. The two Confederate Commissioners on board, John Slidell (right) and James Mason, were taken prisoner and the* Trent *was allowed to proceed. Upon her arrival in England, the British Government was appalled by the apparent Federal disregard of diplomatic immunity. There were a series of meetings between Lord Lyons, the British Minister to the United States, and members of Lincoln's cabinet. Certain ships of the Royal Navy were placed in readiness, but gunboat diplomacy proved unnecessary when the two Commissioners were placed in the custody of Lord Lyons.*

Despite some initial success (notably at the Battle of Bull Run on July 21, 1861), the South seemed overmatched. True, her slender forces soon filled with superb officers and fighting troops. But the South possessed no excessive population of white men of fighting age, still less industrial potential, and her enslaved minority could hardly be counted upon for assistance in the struggle ahead. Then too, the Union's slowly tightening naval blockade threatened to squeeze the South economically dry.

The North, for its part, expected to wage a fairly quick and easy war. Congress authorized drafting 400,000 additional men and spending 400,000,000 additional dollars for the effort. Lincoln's handpicked commanding general — George B. McClellan — began elaborate preparations for a crushing assault.

On November 8, 1861, a United States naval vessel stopped a British passenger ship, the *Trent*, on the high seas in order to detain two American gentlemen. James M. Mason and John Slidell had been on their way to represent the Confederacy in England and France. Their capture boosted Union spirits but it plunged the

President into gloom. The whole episode, Lincoln warned his Cabinet, ran contrary to international law. England now possessed legal justification to invade the United States from Canada, citing the necessity to defend the freedom of the seas.

Indeed, the British retaliated as expected. There was real danger of a two-front war, which would have spelled disaster for the United States. Lincoln, presiding at a stormy Cabinet meeting on Christmas Day, 1861, finally arranged for the two Confederate commissioners to be restored to British protection.

Above: *General Winfield Scott (1786-1866) resigned his command of the Union army for reasons of age. Scott, a hero of the War of 1812 and the Mexican War, found it difficult to deal with younger officers. It took Lincoln two years to find a decent replacement. In the meantime, command of the army was given to General George Brinton McClellan.*

Left: *The first Union troops to answer the call to arms were the Sixth Massachusetts. Four of its soldiers and nine civilians were killed in the mob attack in Baltimore.*

Below: *When Union troops arrived in Washington, the entire city became an armed camp. The Sixth Massachusetts camped in the Senate Chamber and another regiment on the White House lawn.*

Right: *Alfred Waud sketched Lincoln and General Winfield Scott reviewing a three-year regiment in front of the White House in 1861. At that time, some regiments were sworn in for only a year, some for the duration of the conflict. The sketch also shows the White House as it appeared at that time, complete with the statue of Washington on the front lawn.*

LOYAL AMERICANS.

Above: *A popular patriotic engraving of 1861 shows Lincoln and his cabinet. General Scott was still commander of the army at that time. Also pictured are General Anderson, who as a major had commanded the defense of Fort Sumter; General Butler, who had held Baltimore for the Union; and Colonel Ellsworth, the first Union hero, a friend of Lincoln's who was killed when the Federal Army took Alexandria, Virginia.*

Right: *Lincoln kept in close contact with the armies in the field. He is seen here with McClellan and several other generals following the battle of Antietam.*

Above: *Two days of heavy fighting at the Battle of Shiloh, Tennessee, ended in virtual stalemate, but the Federal Army had managed to split the Confederate force along the Mississippi.*

Left: *General Ulysses S. Grant (1822-1885) attended West Point and served in the Mexican War. His civilian career as a shopkeeper in Galena, Illinois, was a dismal failure. At the outbreak of the Civil War, Grant rejoined the army and was quickly promoted to Brigadier General, with a command in the Western Theatre of Operations. His campaigns against Fort Donelson and Fort Henry brought him to Lincoln's notice. Following the capture of Vicksburg and the successful battle of Lookout Mountain, Grant was promoted to the rank of Lieutenant General and made General of the Armies of the United States.*

Above right: *The Union had a tremendous advantage over the South in that most of the manufacturing and casting of weapons, including artillery, was done in the North. The Union arsenal was never empty, while the South was forced to depend on captured weapons and those brought in through the blockade at great expense.*

Below right: *Lincoln met with McClellan several times in the fall of 1862, before replacing him with General Ambrose Burnside. This photograph reveals in some detail the Union officer's campaign furniture: the traveling desk and folding chairs, the woven coverlet, and the captured Confederate flag casually thrown on the ground.*

Above: *The Civil War saw many changes in warfare. Sherman's calculated destruction of the railroads during the March to the Sea increased the difficulty of transporting troops and war materiel, as well as the much needed food throughout the South.*

Right: *By the end of 1864, the war was definitely coming to a close. Thomas Nast sketched Lincoln greeting the Southern States, Robert E. Lee and Jefferson Davis as they return for a united Christmas Dinner. Such allegories were quite popular: this was one of a series published in* Harper's Weekly.

Above: *Certain military inventions saw their first use during the Civil War. Among these were the pontoon bridge and the telegraph, which allowed Lincoln to keep in constant communication with his generals in the field.*

Right: *The Union Army contained several regiments of black soldiers, including 54th Massachusetts, who were best remembered for their gallant attack on Fort Wagner, near Charleston. Before the Emancipation Proclamation, any black wishing to join the army would find himself relegated to road-building, serving white troops, or joining a band. Afterward, black soldiers proved their worth in many battles, including the siege of Petersburg.*

Right: *The fall of Richmond in April 1865 left the former Confederate capital in ruins. The bombardment was followed by a fire, which gutted most of the buildings along the James River and the warehouse near the canal (below).*

Died,

NEAR THE SOUTH-SIDE RAIL ROAD,

ON SUNDAY, APRIL 9th, 1865,

The Southern Confederacy,

AGED FOUR YEARS.

CONCEIVED IN SIN, BORN IN INIQUITY, NURTURED BY TYRANNY, DIED OF
A CHRONIC ATTACK OF PUNCH.

ABRAHAM LINCOLN, Attending Physician.

U. S. GRANT, Undertaker.

JEFF DAVIS, Chief Mourner.

EPITAPH.

Gentle stranger, drop a tear,
The C. S. A. lies buried here:
In youth it lived and prosper'd
   well,
But like Lucifer it fell:
Its body here, its soul in — well
E'en if I knew I wouldn't tell.

Rest C. S. A., from every strife,
Your death is better than your
   life:
And this one line shall grace your
   grave—
Your death gave freedom to the
   slave.

Jas. B. Rodgers, Pr., 52 & 54 North Sixth St
Phila.

Above: *The end of the war was celebrated with a mourning card, similar to those distributed at funerals, or published in the newspapers.*

Right: *General Lee surrendered to General Grant at Appomattox Court House on April 9, 1865. The War was over.*

Far right: *The following June, the Union Army held a Grand Review down Pennsylvania Avenue in Washington before the troops were mustered out.*

Great Britain's ruling class seemed to favor the Confederacy for two reasons. First, the South's gentlemanly plantation-owners were definitely more 'their sort' than the rustic Union president. His funny frontier accent and his rude remarks about 'kingcraft' appeared deplorable to their sensibilities. Second, and more important, England's textile mills were dependent on the South's now unobtainable cotton. However, thanks largely to the massive sales of *Uncle Tom's Cabin* abroad, the British people as a whole were solidly antislavery and pro-Union. That factor, and the death of Prince Albert, combined with Lincoln's astutely prompt surrender of Mason and Slidell, dissuaded England from interfering after all.

Simon Cameron, Lincoln's Secretary of War, had proved personally unfit to administer the Union's mushrooming military affairs. On January 13, 1862, the President replaced Cameron with the man who had once nicknamed Lincoln 'the Giraffe,' and had more recently described him as 'the original gorilla — the Illinois Ape.' Lincoln rightly sensed that Edwin M. Stanton had more to offer than a genius for unkind epithets. This hard-driving little man could bring force and competence to the conduct of the war.

The President related an anecdote concerning a preacher out West whose parishioners put rocks in his pockets to keep him on the earth. 'We may be obliged to serve Stanton in the same way,' Lincoln remarked, 'but I guess we'll let him jump a while first.'

Arrogant and obnoxious though he was, Stanton jumped as promised. 'As soon as I can get the machinery of the office working, the rats cleared out, and the rat holes stopped,' he promised, 'we shall move! This army has got to fight or run away.... The champagne and oysters on the Potomac must be stopped.' He was as good as his word. Like Secretary Seward, Stanton also grew remarkably under pressure. These two men became Lincoln's staunchest civilian allies.

Borrowing military textbooks from the Library of Congress, Lincoln studied far into the night. He played an extremely active role in the entire conduct of the war. Meanwhile, however, he had to deal with happy distractions and with tragedies as well on the home front.

Far left: *Edwin M. Stanton (1814-1869) was Lincoln's second Secretary of War. A lawyer born in Ohio, Stanton, a Democrat, had served the Buchanan Administration as Attorney General. After his appointment as Secretary of War, he made radical changes in the War Department, clearing up much of the fraud and influence-peddling that had plagued that office. A severe critic at the outset, he ended up as one of Lincoln's staunchest admirers.*

Left: *Mary Lincoln also sat for photographs by Mathew Brady. This likeness, which she herself pronounced 'excellent,' has been retouched to make her slimmer. The* St. Louis Missouri Democrat, *in describing the new First Lady, observed that: 'She displayed but little jewelry and this was well and appropriately adjusted. She is a lady of fine figure and accomplished address and is well calculated to grace and do honor at the White House.'*

Young Robert Lincoln was away at Harvard now, but young Tad and Willie had the run of the White House. They rigged up its flat roof like the deck of a ship, from which to spy out and defeat enemy cruisers. They collected more than a dozen pets. They pulled bellcords at random to send staff members scurrying in all directions. Playing war, they planned to execute and bury one of their dolls for having slept on picket duty, but their father for once intervened. Lincoln sent a hasty note out to the garden: 'The doll Jack is pardoned. By order of the President.'

Lincoln frequently pardoned actual soldiers as well. Stanton and various generals complained that this was bad for discipline, yet the President persisted in so doing throughout the war. 'Do you see these papers crowded into these pigeonholes?' he once said to a visitor. 'They are the cases that you call by that long title, "cowardice in the face of the enemy," but I call them, for short, my "leg cases." But I put it to you, and I leave it to you to decide for youself: if Almighty God gives a man a cowardly pair of legs, how can he help their running away with him?'

In February 1862, young Willie died at the White House after a brief illness. The Lincolns were grief-stricken, and for a few weeks the President seemed to ignore the war. 'Do you ever find yourself talking with the dead?' Lincoln asked Secretary of the Treasury Salmon Chase. 'I do. Ever since Willie's death I find myself involuntarily talking with him as if he were with me — and I feel that he is!'

The Lincolns, in their distress, invited spiritualist mediums to conduct seances at the White House — with predictably blurred results. This prompted public doubts and journalistic attacks upon Lincoln's competence, including one anonymous pamphlet entitled: *The Nation Demoralized and its President a Spirit Rapper.*

Far left: *This photograph of Lincoln and his youngest son, Tad, was a popular one, and many artists used it as the basis of paintings and woodcuts.*

Above: *Robert Todd Lincoln, the oldest son, was a student at Harvard when his father was elected President.*

Left: *Mary Lincoln wearing mourning for her son Willie, who died in 1862 at the age of 11.*

Mary Todd Lincoln had lavishly refurbished the White House at public expense, and done all that was in her power to make it Washington's social center. But the Capital's old-line 'cliff-dwellers' scorned, snubbed and despised the jealous, overdressed, hysteria-prone First Lady from Illinois. The onetime belle whose relatives had regarded Lincoln as a vulgar, unworthy swain, now found herself subject to general ridicule.

Wasting a whole year in command (November 1, 1861 — November 5, 1862) General McClellan inconclusively thrust and parried against the South's numerically inferior but more experienced armies. In June his roundabout Peninsular Campaign, which Lincoln had always distrusted, bogged down short of the Confederate Capital Richmond, Virginia. On September 17, 1862, McClellan did finally prevail at the bloody battle of Antietam, Maryland. But he neglected to follow up his victory.

Lincoln had badly overestimated this West Pointer. McClellan possessed far more impressive horsemanship and sense of his own importance than he had force of character. Why did Lincoln wait so long to relieve him? Perhaps the President already guessed that McClellan's most prestigious rivals and obvious replacements — Pope, Burnside, Hooker, Halleck, Meade — would also prove themselves inferior to the South's brilliant commanders.

About the time that he removed McClellan, the President wrote a poignant, undated memorandum to himself. His personal secretary, John Hay, preserved it:

'In great contests each party claims to act in accordance with the will of God. Both may be, and one must be, wrong. God cannot be for and against the same thing at the same time. In the present civil war it is quite possible that God's purpose is something different from the purpose of either party.... By His mere great power on the minds of the now contestants, He could have either saved or destroyed the Union without a human contest. Yet the contest began. And, having begun, He could give the final victory to either side any day. Yet the contest proceeds.'

Though the greater part of Lincoln's time and energy was taken up with the war, a number of bills on non-military matters were passed by Congress, with far reaching results. Among these was the Homestead Act of 1862 which granted 160-acre quarter sections of land to anyone for a nominal fee, plus five years residence and improvements on the property. This was a critical step to the settlement and development of the western territories, as was the Morril Land Grant Act of 1862 which gave states apportionments of public land to build agricultural colleges. Lincoln, remembering his own hardscrabble childhood and unslakened thirst for education, was aware this new law would alleviate similar yearnings in young people on other frontiers.

Far left: *A posed photograph of Mary Lincoln in the gown she wore for one of the inaugural balls gives some impression of the graceful Southern belle who had charmed Lincoln almost twenty years before.*

Left: *Lincoln, with an office seeker carrying one of the soon-to-be notorious carpetbags, was sketched by David Hunter Strother in 1864.*

On January 1, 1863, Lincoln issued the Emancipation Proclamation, which states 'all persons held as slaves within said designated States and parts of States, are, and henceforth shall be, free.' In one way the fierce battle that had waged since the Missouri Compromise of 1820 was finished, but the war was still to be won.

To maintain the size of the army, the Senate and then the House of Representatives passed the conscription act of 1862 calling for the enlistment of all able-bodied male citizens between the ages of 20 and 45. By this time both the Confederacy and the Union were aware that the war was no picnic. Several times during the war Lincoln would agree to a general amnesty to encourage deserters to return to their regiments.

Throughout the war other issues continued to compete for Lincoln's attention. There were Indian uprisings in Minnesota, which resulted in 39 tribesmen being executed. Lincoln also took time to meet with members of other Indian tribes, advising them to give up their traditional nomadic ways for 'the cultivation of the earth to provide economic stability for their people.'

During the spring of 1863, rebel forces commanded by Robert E. Lee, surged up into Pennsylvania. During the first three days of July, in one of the war's bloodiest battles, they were barely turned back at Gettysburg. The final Confederate initiative had ended. Now they would be forced to fight a defensive war.

On November 19, 1863, Lincoln delivered a brief speech at the dedication of the war cemetery at the Gettysburg battlefield. He had written it out on a single sheet — not the back of an envelope as legend insists — that very morning. It caused no particular stir at the time. That was reserved for the oration by Edward Everett, the guest speaker. But Lincoln's brief address has no peer in American political literature, except the Declaration of Independence.

Far left: *Edward Everett, the noted politician and orator, was chosen to give the address at the dedication of the military cemetery on the Battlefield of Gettysburg in 1863.*

Below: *Lincoln (seated in the center of the picture) gave a short speech at the end of Everett's oration. In ten short sentences, he immortalized the battle and those who fought it.*

At the end of his annual message to Congress that year, Lincoln made a statement on the steps to reconstruction following what he felt would be the inevitable Union victory. It is interesting for its fairness, and for the contrast to the Reconstruction that did take place following Lincoln's assassination. The proclamation promised full pardon to all Confederates except government officials, high-ranking officers, those who had resigned from the U.S. military service, and those who had mistreated prisoners, white or black. Furthermore, it pledged the return of all property, except, of course, slaves; it made pardons conditional on an oath of allegiance to the United States; and it allowed former Confederate states to return to Federal statehood if a tenth of the citizens would swear allegiance and forswear slavery. Lincoln's whole proposal for reconstruction was met with widespread approval. However the House of Representatives later passed a bill suggesting harshly punitive measures be taken against the defeated side, and some even more radical Republicans felt then that, the Wade-Davis Reconstruction Bill, was not harsh enough. Lincoln vetoed the bill when it reached his desk, and continued to press for more magnanimous treatment. It is a pity that in the heat of revenge following his assassination, no one thought to honor his memory by following his wishes.

Back in Washington, Lincoln kept close watch on his troops, marking their positions on the war maps which covered the walls of his White House office. The Union campaigns, especially those conducted by a fast-rising officer in the West, Ulysses S. Grant, were becoming more and more successful.

On July 3, 1863, Grant had captured Vicksburg, the last remaining Confederate position on the Mississippi. 'The Father of Waters goes unvexed to the sea!' Lincoln exulted. Earlier, at Shiloh Church, in southern Tennessee, Grant had accepted 13,000 casualties to gain the victory. Some said he ought to be removed for drunkenness, but Lincoln disagreed. 'I can't spare this man,' the President said simply. 'He fights.'

Lincoln summoned Grant to Washington for consultation. Together they worked out a strategy for engaging the South simultaneously on every front. 'Those not skinning can hold a leg,' Lincoln grimly remarked, and Grant was delighted. Lincoln later said that he regarded Grant as 'The first general I have had. You know how it has been with all the rest.'

On March 10, 1864, Lincoln elevated Grant to supreme commander. This cool, relentless campaigner, abetted by William Tecumseh Sherman, soon had the whole South reeling in confusion and retreat.

The North's previous frustrations and defeats had badly eroded Lincoln's popularity. Even within his own Republican ranks, many thought that the President possessed no chance of being re-elected President. But Grant's advances in Virginia and Sherman's capture of Atlanta changed the picture.

Above: *The Emancipation Proclamation was one of the most important pieces of legislation to come out of the Lincoln Administration. Lincoln discussed it at length with his cabinet.*

Right: *The various symbols scattered through a print of Lincoln writing the Emancipation Proclamation include the scales of justice out of balance, the bust of Buchanan in a noose, and the copies of the Bible and Constitution on Lincoln's knee.*

Winning his party's nomination after all, Lincoln was re-elected by a near-landslide vote on the eighth of November, 1864. His disappointed Democratic opponent was none other than General McClellan.

In his capacity as wartime Commander-in-Chief, Lincoln had already issued a Proclamation of Emancipation of the slaves. Now was the time to make slavery forever more anathema in the United States, he urged Congress, by means of a 13th Amendment to the Constitution itself. Reminding reluctant Congressmen that he had just received a vast popular mandate, Lincoln lobbied hard for this Amendment. 'If slavery is not wrong,' he explained simply, 'nothing is wrong.' The Amendment passed, but by an uncomfortably slender majority: 119 to 58.

Below: *Cartoonist Adalbert Volck, a southern sympathizer, viewed it differently. Here the influence of the devil and drink seems to inspire the writer, while the Constitution is trodden upon.*

Left: *Posters and prints of the Emancipation Proclamation, suitable for framing, were soon available.*

Right: *After the fall of Richmond, Lincoln went to view the conquered city. He visited the Confederate White House, whose former occupant, Jefferson Davis, had fled to Danville, Virginia. He would not be captured until May.*

Below right: *The day after Lee's surrender the front page of the* New York Times *included copies of the correspondence between Grant and Lee.*

Below far right: *Lincoln was acclaimed by black freedmen wherever he walked during the trip to Richmond.*

Nonetheless, as the President declared, this was a 'great moral victory' which no one could ever take away. In one of his rare jovial moods, Lincoln stepped to his office window and pointed south across the Potomac. 'If the people over the river had behaved themselves,' he confessed with a ghost of a smile,' I could never have done what I have.'

But if the ultimate extirpation of slavery was sweet, the Union's looming victory promised to produce an overflowing measure of bitterness. The President dreaded the time of vengeance to come. With melancholy prescience, he saw that the southern states lay under threat of savage reprisal from the long-bloodied North. He continued to press for peaceful reconstruction, even in his second inaugural address:

'with malice toward none, with charity for all.'

Following his Second Inauguration in March, Lincoln hurried to the front to suggest Grant and Sherman prepare to accept surrender of the South's armed forces — at least — in a generous, non-vindictive spirit.

As Grant was to recall it, Lincoln 'spent the last days of his life with me.... He came down to City Point in the last days of the war, and was with me the whole time... He was incontestably the greatest man I ever knew.'

At Appomattox Courthouse, Virginia, on April 9, 1865, Grant kept a final — peaceful — appointment with his long elusive opponent: Robert E. Lee. The surrender terms which he set down for Lee's forces were tempered with justice and mercy for all.

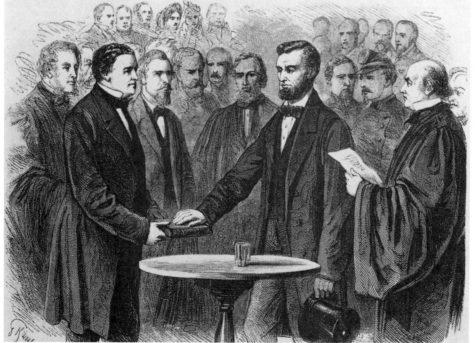

Above: *On March 4, 1865, Lincoln took the oath of office for the second time. Knowing that the end of the war was in sight, Lincoln spoke of making peace: '... with malice toward none; with charity for all; with firmness in the right, as God gives us to see the right, let us strive on to finish the work we are in: to bind up the nation's wounds; to care for him who shall have borne the battle, and for his widow and orphan — to do all which may achieve and cherish a just and lasting peace, among ourselves, and with all nations.'*

Left: *This time the oath of office was administered by the new Chief Justice, Salmon Chase.*

BILL OF FARE

OF THE

Presidential Inauguration Ball

IN THE

CITY OF WASHINGTON, D. C.,

On the 6th of March 1865.

Oyster Stews . . . .
Terrapin " . . . .
Oysters, pickled . . . .

BEEF.

Roast Beef . . . .
Filet de Beef . . . .
Beef à-la-mode . . . .
Beef à l'anglais . . . .

VEAL.

Leg of Veal . . . .
Fricandeau . . . .
Veal Malakoff . . . .

POULTRY.

Roast Turkey . . . .
Boned " . . . .
Roast Chicken . . . .
Grouse, boned and roast . . . .

GAME.

Pheasant . . . .
Quail . . . .
Venison . . . .

PATETES.

Patête of Duck en gelée . . . .
Patête de fois gras . . . .

SMOKED.

Ham . . . .
Tongue en gelée . . . .
do plain . . . .

SALADES.

Chicken . . . .
Lobster . . . .

Ornamental Pyramides.

Nougate . . . .
Orange . . . .
Caramel with Fancy Cream Candy
Cocoanut . . . .
Macaroon . . . .

Croquant . . . .
Chocolate . . . .
Tree Cakes . . . .

CAKES AND TARTS.

Almond Sponge . . . .
Belle Alliance . . . .
Dame Blanche . . . .
Macaroon Tart . . . .
Tart à la Nelson . . . .
Tarte à l'Orleans . . . .
do à la Portugaise . . . .
do à la Vienne . . . .
Pound Cake . . . .
Sponge Cake . . . .
Lady Cake . . . .
Fancy small Cakes . . . .

JELLIES AND CREAMS.

Calfsfoot and Wine Jelly . . . . .
Charlotte à la Russe . . . .
do do Vanilla . . . .
Blanc Mangue . . . .
Crême Neapolitane . . . .
do à la Nelson . . . .
do Chateaubriand . . . .
do à la Smyrna . . . .
do do Nesselrode . . . .
Bombe à la Vanilla . . . .

ICE CREAM.

Vanilla . . . .
Lemon . . . .
White Coffee . . . .
Chocolate . . . .
Burnt Almonds . . . .
Maraschino . . . .

FRUIT ICES.

Strawberry . . . .
Orange . . . .
Lemon . . . .

DESSERT.

Grapes, Almonds, Raisins, &c.

Coffee and Chocolate.

Furnished by **G. A. BALZER**, CONFECTIONER,
Cor. 9th & D Sts., Washington, D. C.

Above: *The Inaugural festivities were a delight to Mrs. Lincoln, but bored the President. As usual during the war, men in uniform were plentiful, and certain members of the cabinet, including Secretary Stanton and Lincoln's new Vice-President, Andrew Johnson, were also present.*

Left: *The menu for the Inaugural Ball proves that the deprivations suffered by the South were not shared by the North.*

Five days later, on the evening of Friday, April 14, a mad actor named John Wilkes Booth slipped silently into the Presidential box at Ford's Theatre in Washington. Lincoln and Mary sat there with friends, enjoying Laura Keene's performance in a hit comedy called *Our American Cousin.*

Booth fired a fatal bullet into the back of Lincoln's head. Then, leaping down to the stage (and breaking a leg in the process), the histrionic assassin cried out the motto of the state of Virginia: *Sic semper tyrannis!* ('Thus always to tyrants!').

The President was taken to a house across the street, where he died the following day in the presence of his son, Robert, and others, including Secretary Stanton. The man who had once insulted Lincoln by calling him the Illinois Ape, had changed his opinion when it came time to announce the President's death. 'Now,' said Stanton, 'Now he belongs to the ages.'

Above and top right: *Lincoln's assassin was a well-known actor with Southern sympathies, John Wilkes Booth. After that April evening, many saw him as the tool of the devil.*

Right: *Lincoln was carried across the street to a modest house belonging to a tailor named William Peterson. It was here that he died the following morning.*

Top: *Booth shot Lincoln in the presidential box at Ford's Theater, where the Lincolns were entertaining friends and enjoying Laura Keene in* Our American Cousin. *Booth had first schemed to kidnap the president and hold him as a hostage for the release of certain Confederate prisoners.*

Above: *Booth was only one member of this conspiracy. The others, including Lewis Payne, who stabbed Secretary of State William Seward, were captured and hanged at the Old Penitentiary in Washington on July 7, 1865.*

155

Throughout the days of mourning that followed, during the lying-in-state in the White House, and the long sad train journey back to Springfield, there would be an outpouring of grief. Many would stand in silence, bareheaded to watch the funeral train pass, there would be stops in major cities to allow stunned citizens to view the body, and much poetry good and bad would be written. Walt Whitman's *When the Lilacs Last in the Dooryard Bloom'd* and *O Captain, my Captain* were written in Lincoln's memory, as was *Sail on, sail on, O Ship of State* by Henry Longfellow. But perhaps the best epitaph of all is to be found on the face of the Lincoln penny. The border above Lincoln's profile carries the words, *'In God We Trust.'* To the left at the Great Emancipator's back, we find the single word — *'Liberty.'*

Left: *This familiar image of Lincoln was one of the two that inspired Victor Brenner in 1909 when he modeled the Lincoln penny.*

Above: *Andrew Johnson (1808-1875) had been Vice-President for only six weeks when Lincoln was assassinated. He tried to carry out Lincoln's plans for Reconstruction, but was balked by those who thirsted for revenge.*

Columbia's noblest Sons

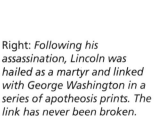

Right: *Following his assassination, Lincoln was hailed as a martyr and linked with George Washington in a series of apotheosis prints. The link has never been broken.*

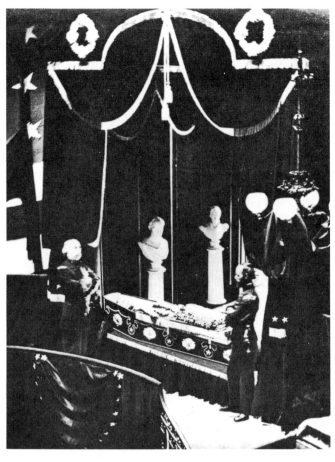

For the reunified nation, there was mourning. Lincoln's body was taken back to Springfield by train for burial. Along the way, the body lay in state in New York, Chicago and other large cities, to allow the grieving public to pay their last respects. Many stood in the rain to watch the funeral train on its slow, sad journey.

INDEX

Picture Credits

Bison Picture Library: 90, 123 top.
Chicago Historical Society: 2-3, 16, 72, 132 bottom, 137 top.
Cincinnati Art Museum: 99.
Culver Pictures: 8-9.
John Hay Library, Brown University: 27, 42, 52, 53 top, 70, 73, 82, 83, 84-85, 86, 87, 88-89, 91, 92-93, 94 top and bottom, 95, 100 top, 101 bottom, 105, 106 left and right, 107, 109, 110, 116, 118, 120, 134 bottom, 18 top, 145, 149 top, 156 bottom.
Illinois State Historical Library: 21, 23 top, 26 bottom, 140, 154 top right, 157 top left.
Kurtz and Allison: 96 top.
Library of Congress: 10, 11, 14-15, 18, 26 top, 30, 32, 33, 34-35, 36, 37, 44, 45, 46-47, 48, 53 bottom, 54, 56 top and bottom, 58, 59, 61, 62, 63, 64,

65 top and bottom, 67, 68-69, 74, 75, 76, 78, 79, 97, 100 bottom, 101 top, 102-103, 108, 111 bottom, 113, 114-115, 121 top, 123 bottom, 124, 125, 126, 128 top and bottom, 129 top, 130, 132 top, 133 top and bottom, 134 top, 135 bottom, 136-137, 138 bottom, 139, 143 bottom, 146, 147, 149 bottom, 150, 151 bottom left, 152 bottom, 153 bottom, 155 all, 156 top, 157 top right.
The Metropolitan Museum of Art: 50.
National Archives: 1, 7, 13, 40-41, 49, 50-51, 77, 104, 112, 127, 131, 135 top, 142, 143 top, 148, 151 top and bottom right, 152 top, 153 top, 154 bottom right, 156 left.
Naval History Photograph: 47 top.
New York Historical Society: 57.

New York Public Library: 60 (The Arents Collection), 81 top.
Railroad Museum of Pennsylvania: 157 bottom.
University of Nebraska: 68
Virginia State Library: 4-5, 111 top.
Louis A. Warren Lincoln Library and Museum: 12, 22, 23 bottom, 25, 29, 38, 43, 66, 121 bottom, 122, 141, 144, 154 left.

The author and publishers would like to thank the following people for their help: Michael Rose for the design, Mary Raho for the picture research, Elizabeth Montgomery for the editing, Gisela Knight for the index and Jennifer Lee at the John Hay Library, Brown University.